THE PLAIN-ENGLISH GUIDE TO ECONOMIC SANCTIONS: THE COMPLETE SERIES

By Heidi Hunter

St. Paul, Minnesota

The Plain-English Guide to Economic Sanctions: The Complete Series

Copyright © 2025 Heidi Hunter

First Edition: March 2025

All rights reserved. No part of this book may be reproduced in any form or by any electronic or mechanical means, including information storage and retrieval systems, without permission in writing from the publisher, except by reviewers, who may quote brief passages in a review. The author expressly prohibits any entity from using this publication to train artificial intelligence (AI) technologies to generate text, including, without limitation, technologies capable of generating works in the same style or genre as this publication. The author reserves all rights to license the use of this work for generative AI training and development of machine learning language models.

Published by LilAbby Press
St. Paul, Minnesota
Printed in the United States of America

ISBN: 979-8-9921409-5-8 (e-book)
ISBN: 979-8-9921409-6-5 (paperback)

cover design by Heidi Hunter

Table of Contents

Disclaimer 1
Introduction 2
Definitions 5
INTRODUCTION TO ECONOMIC SANCTIONS 14
1 Introduction to Economic Sanctions 15
2 How Economic Sanctions Are Created 17
3 Who Has To Comply with Economic Sanctions? 20
4 Types of Economic Sanctions 25
5 How Economic Sanctions Affect Your Job and Your Company 31
SETTING UP AN ECONOMIC SANCTIONS COMPLIANCE PROGRAM (SCP) 34
6 How Do I Comply with Economic Sanctions? 35
7 Sanctions Compliance Officer/Responsible Party 36
8 Economic Sanctions Policy 38
9 Written Sanctions Procedures 43
10 Setting Up a Scanning Program 46
11 Due Diligence 57
12 Sanctions Clauses 61
13 Environmental Scanning 65
14 Training 68
15 Auditing/Testing 73
CONDUCTING A RISK ASSESSMENT 76
16 Introduction to Risk Assessments 77
17 Steps in the Risk Assessment Process 79
18 Scoping 80
19 Risk Categories 83
20 Sanctions Risks 92
21 Risk Criteria 94
22 Risk Scores 97
23 Assessing Risks 98
24 Identify Controls 105

25 Assess Controls 109
26 Gap Identification and Remediation 113
27 Risk Assessment Documentation and Next Steps 116
HOW TO HANDLE SANCTIONED PARTIES AND TRANSACTIONS 117
28 What if My Customer Is Sanctioned? 118
29 Can I Do Any Business with Sanctioned Parties or Countries? 124
OTHER SANCTIONS CONSIDERATIONS 129
30 Documentation 130
31 What Are the Penalties for Non-Compliance? 131
32 Are Sanctions the Same in Every Country? 133
33 Economic Sanctions Nuances 135
34 Managing US Parent Versus Foreign Branch or Subsidiary Conflicts 140
35 Trade Sanctions 143
36 What's New in Sanctions for 2025 146
ADDITIONAL INSURANCE COMPANY CONSIDERATIONS FOR SANCTIONS 149
37 Economic Sanctions Considerations for Insurance 150
38 Insurance Matters Complicating Sanctions Compliance 155
39 Specific Issues by Insurance Product 161
40 Conclusion 165
41 Test Your Knowledge 167
References 176
Author Biography 179
All Books in the Plain-English Guide Series by Heidi Hunter 180
Notes 181

Disclaimer

The information provided in this book is for informational purposes only and is not intended to constitute legal advice. The author of this book is not an attorney, is not providing legal advice, and is not creating an attorney-client relationship with the reader.

Readers should not act or rely on any information in this book without seeking the advice of a lawyer. Any reliance upon the information contained in this guide is solely at the reader's own risk.

The author makes no representations or warranties about the completeness, accuracy, reliability, or suitability of the information in this book.

While every effort has been made to provide accurate and complete guidance, it's critical to understand that this guide does not guarantee an effective sanctions compliance program free from fines or penalties. Compliance with economic sanctions regulations is a complex and evolving area, and the effectiveness of any program depends on various factors, including the specific circumstances of the reader's business and the actions of relevant regulatory authorities. Therefore, the author cannot guarantee specific outcomes or results from implementing the suggestions provided in this guide. This information is a tool to develop and enhance your sanctions compliance program, but the ultimate responsibility for compliance rests with the reader and their organization.

In no event shall the author be liable for any loss or damage whatsoever arising from, or in connection with, the use of the information contained in this book.

Introduction

Economic sanctions are powerful tools governments and international bodies use to influence the behavior of nations, organizations, and individuals. Navigating the complex sanctions landscape can be challenging for businesses—big or small, domestic or international.

That's why I created *The Plain-English Guide to Economic Sanctions: The Complete Series*. This book combines insights from my five prior guides into one updated, easy-to-read resource.

The Complete Series includes content from:
- *The Plain-English Guide to Economic Sanctions*
- *The Plain-English Guide to Developing an Economic Sanctions Program*
- *The Plain-English Guide to Economic Sanctions Risk Assessments*
- *The Plain-English Guide to Economic Sanctions for Insurance Companies*
- *The Plain-English Guide to Economic Sanctions for Foreign Companies*

This updated guide includes fresh examples and the latest developments in sanctions to keep you informed and ahead of the curve.

This book is designed to provide a clear understanding of economic sanctions, how they impact you, what steps you can take to comply with them, and details on implementing a sanctions compliance program and conducting a sanctions risk assessment. It is aimed at practitioners of all levels and uses real-world examples and practical tips for sanctions compliance.

What You'll Gain

You'll benefit from this guide by:

- Gaining a clear understanding of US economic sanctions enforced by the Office of Foreign Assets Control (OFAC) and their global impact.
- Learning how US economic sanctions work and when they apply to foreign companies.

- Navigating the legal frameworks and complexities of OFAC sanctions.
- Developing, strengthening, or refining an effective sanctions compliance program tailored to your business.
- Following step-by-step guidance on conducting risk assessments to identify and mitigate exposure.
- Receiving industry-specific insights, such as the insurance industry, with real-world examples to drive the points home.
- Protecting your organization's reputation and avoiding costly penalties through ethical compliance.
- Discovering key strategies and best practices for navigating economic sanctions successfully.

This guide will mainly focus on economic sanctions enforced by the Office of Foreign Assets Control (OFAC). You'll see terms like "economic sanctions," "OFAC sanctions," "trade sanctions," "sanctions regulations," "OFAC regulations," and "US sanctions" used interchangeably—they all refer to the same thing. We'll also touch on other sanctions managed by agencies like the Department of State and the Bureau of Industry and Security. Since many businesses operate globally, we'll also compare OFAC sanctions with those from major economies like the UK and EU and provide guidance on how foreign companies can comply with OFAC.

Why It Matters

Sanctions compliance isn't just about avoiding fines (though those can be substantial). It's also about protecting your business's reputation, maintaining customer trust, and operating ethically in a complex global environment. Violations can lead to multi-million-dollar civil and criminal penalties,[1] damage your brand, and invite scrutiny from regulators and business partners. By understanding these risks, you can take the necessary steps to safeguard your company and navigate the sanctions landscape with confidence.

Who This Guide Is For

Whether you're a seasoned compliance professional, a new employee, a business owner wearing multiple hats, or someone just trying to make sense of sanctions, this guide breaks it down in simple terms. By the end, you'll have the knowledge and tools to confidently navigate this complex area and build a stronger, more secure future for your business.

The recommendations in this guide draw on the author's experience, industry standards, and OFAC compliance guidance.

Definitions

Some of the terms referenced in this guide are defined below.

Additional Insureds

Someone other than the policyholder is covered under the policy. This can include branches, subsidiaries, employees or directors, or counterparties with an interest in the policy.

Beneficial Owner

The person who ultimately owns, benefits from, or controls an asset.

Beneficiary

The person or entity legally designated to receive the benefits of a financial product such as life insurance.

Blocking Program

An OFAC sanctions program that requires a sanctioned party's assets to be blocked or frozen. US persons are prohibited from doing business with them.

Bureau of Industry and Security (BIS)

The US Department of Commerce's Bureau of Industry and Security (BIS) administers and enforces export controls on dual-use and certain munitions items.

Bordereau(x)

A report sent by an insurance company to its reinsurer listing policies covered or claims paid under the reinsurance contract. There are premium bordereaux and claims bordereaux.

Business Partner/Third Party

Any external party you do business with. A business partner can be a vendor, a subcontractor, an attorney, a joint venture partner, a consultant, a distributor or wholesaler, a supplier, or an agent or representative acting on a company's behalf.

Claimant

The person or entity that requests payment from an insurance company for a loss covered by a policy. The claimant could be the named insured, or it could be a third party seeking compensation.

Comprehensive Sanctions

A trade embargo against a country. Most transactions are prohibited. Countries under comprehensive sanctions are Iran, Cuba, Syria[2], North Korea, and Russian-held areas of Ukraine, such as Crimea.

Control Gap

An internal control either does not exist or does not function properly.

Correspondent Banking

A US financial institution acts as a middleman for a foreign financial institution, giving them access to the US banking system through a single account. Generally, a foreign bank will conduct all customer transactions through this account.

Debt/Equity Restrictions

OFAC restricts the issuance of long-term debt (with terms over fourteen or thirty days, for example) or the purchase of equity for some non-SDN parties. "Debt" includes bonds, loans, extensions of credit, loan guarantees, letters of credit, discount notes or bills, or commercial paper, while equity includes stocks and shares.[3]

Department of State (DoS)

The Department of State has several divisions that oversee the export of defense-related items and services and weapons of mass destruction.

Directive

A Directive is a determination by the President that certain activity is prohibited under an Executive Order. There might be limits on debt or equity, import/export restrictions, or restrictions on specific sectors such as energy, defense, and finance.

Dual-Use Goods

Goods, software, and technology that can be used for both civilian and military purposes.

Economic Sanctions

The government's restrictions or penalties on individuals, entities, groups, governments, or countries to achieve particular foreign policy or national security goals.

Environmental Scanning

Also known as e-scanning. Environmental scanning is how you, as the sanctions compliance professional, stay updated on changes in economic sanctions regulations.

Executive Order

When the President wants to impose new economic sanctions, he will issue an Executive Order. The Executive Order explains why sanctions are needed, the laws under which the Executive Order is created, and who can be sanctioned under the program.

Facilitation

Assisting others in conducting a transaction that violates sanctions if you had conducted it yourself.

Freezing or Blocking Assets

Preventing a sanctioned party from accessing or using assets you hold that belong to them, such as a bank account or an insurance policy. Assets are deposited into a blocked bank account when possible.

Foreign Company

In this guide, a foreign company refers to any entity neither located in nor registered to do business in the United States.

Fuzzy Logic

A sanctions screening application that employs fuzzy logic uses variations in spelling, phonetics, and name transposition (switching of first and last names, for example) to determine a possible match.

Indirect

Selling goods or services to someone acting on behalf of a sanctioned party or country.

Internal Controls

Internal controls are the processes, procedures, and measures that prevent and detect sanctions violations.

List-Based Sanctions

Programs where sanctioned parties are added to the Specially Designated Nationals (SDN) list. Most transactions with them are prohibited, and assets you hold that belong to them may need to be blocked.

Lloyd's Syndicate

The Lloyd's Syndicate in the UK allows multiple insurance companies to share risks for large or high-risk policies. Insurers can be the lead on a policy or a tier or follow the lead of another insurer on a tier.

Nexus

Transactions connected to the US, such as participation by a US party, sale of a US good or service, and transacting in US dollars or through the US financial system. Non-US persons carrying out a transaction outside the US may be required to comply with US sanctions if that transaction has a US nexus.

The term is also used when referencing whether a particular transaction, claim, or policy has a connection to a sanctioned country, party, or good.

Office of Foreign Assets Control (OFAC)

The Office of Foreign Assets Control (OFAC), part of the US Department of the Treasury, oversees most US sanctions programs.

OFAC Regulations

OFAC incorporates sanctions laws and executive orders into its own regulations for a program, which are issued in the Code of Federal Regulations (CFR). The CFR is where all rules implemented by the Federal government are published.

OFAC Sanctions

Sanctions administered by the Office of Foreign Assets Control (OFAC). You'll see terms like "economic sanctions," "OFAC sanctions," "trade sanctions," "sanctions regulations," "OFAC regulations," and "US sanctions" used interchangeably in this guide.

Policyholder

The individual or entity who purchases and owns the policy. They are listed as the primary insured in a policy.

Politically Exposed Person (PEP)

Foreign individuals who are or have been entrusted with a prominent public function, as well as their immediate family members and close associates.[4]

Possible Match/False Positive/Positive Match

A possible match occurs when your sanctions screening system determines your customer may be a match to a person on the SDN list. A possible or potential match is also known as an "alert" or a "hit." "Possible match," "potential match," "alert," and "hit" are used interchangeably within this guide.

A false positive is a hit, which, after reviewing additional information on the customer and sanctioned party, is not an actual match. A positive match, on the other hand, is an alert that is determined to be an actual match once your customer's information is compared to the sanctioned party's information.

Risk Assessment

A risk assessment is a method for identifying, analyzing, and addressing a company's sanctions risks. It pinpoints any weaknesses in the program and lays out a plan to fix them.

Risk Category

Groups of similar types of risks, such as customers, products, services, geography, transactions, and third parties.

Risk Criteria

The measures used to evaluate the significance of a risk. They include inherent risk, residual risk, likelihood, and severity.

Risk Score

A categorical value (high, medium, and low) is assigned to a risk based on its assessed impact and likelihood. This score helps prioritize which risks need immediate attention and action.

Root Cause

The root cause is the main reason why a process failed.

Sanctions Compliance Officer (SCO)

The person within an organization with ultimate responsibility for the sanctions compliance program.

Sanctions Compliance Program (SCP)

A sanctions compliance program (SCP) is the policies, procedures, and controls that help companies comply with sanctions regulations.

Sanctions Compliance/Sanctions Compliance Team

Sanctions compliance is the function within a company responsible for managing the policy, program, and controls related to sanctions compliance. The SCO is part of this function. This function may also include a separate team dedicated to sanctions (i.e., the Sanctions Compliance Team).

Sanctions Evasion

Sanctions evasion occurs when people try to structure a transaction to get around sanctions.

Sanctions Program

A sanctions program consists of all the laws, Executive Orders, OFAC regulations, guidance, licenses, and frequently asked questions related to restrictions against a specific country or activity. It governs what you can and cannot do.

Sanctions Risk

Sanctions risk refers to potential threats or weaknesses that, if not properly managed by internal controls, can result in violations of OFAC's regulations.

Scanning/Screening

Reviewing a customer or transaction to see if there is a potential sanctions issue. This can involve scanning a customer or payee name against OFAC's watchlists or reviewing a transaction for a sanctions nexus.

Sectoral Sanctions

Sectoral sanctions prohibit certain activities in targeted industries with designated entities, while any other activity is legal.

Secondary Sanctions

Also known as "extraterritorial sanctions." Under certain programs, like those related to Iran or Russia, non-US persons can face penalties under US law for prohibited activities, even if they have no ties, connection, or nexus to the US. Additionally, US entities will be prohibited from engaging in transactions with these penalized parties.

Specially Designated National (SDN)/Sanctioned Party

An individual, company, organization, group, government, vessel, or aircraft sanctioned by OFAC and listed on the Specially Designated Nationals (SDN) list. Their assets are blocked, and US persons are generally prohibited from dealing with them.[5]

The 50 Percent Rule

Entities majority-owned (50 percent or more) by one or more blocked persons, either through direct or indirect ownership, are also considered sanctioned despite not being named on a watchlist.

Threshold

A threshold is the level at which the sanctions screening application considers a person a potential match to a sanctioned party. One hundred percent generally means an exact name match. Lower thresholds (such as 95 percent) mean it is a possible match based on fuzzy logic. For example, your customer "Jose C. Rodriguez" may match against "Jose Rodrigues" or "Jose P Rodriguez" at a 95 percent threshold.

US Person

US citizens anywhere in the world, US-incorporated businesses, including their foreign branches, people who are in the US for any reason, even if they are citizens of another country, and any persons transacting in the US financial system, US dollars, or US goods.

US-Origin Goods

A good is considered of US origin if it is "all or virtually all" made in the United States. The origin refers to where the product was produced or manufactured, not where it was shipped from. Goods located in or passing through the US are also considered US origin. Foreign-made goods containing at least 25 percent US-origin content (10 percent for certain countries) or those directly made from US technology or software are also classified as US origin.

Watchlists

Watchlists are lists maintained by OFAC of sanctioned parties. These lists can be Specially Designated Nationals (SDN) and non-SDN lists. These lists specify various prohibitions against sanctioned parties, from complete asset and transaction bans (for those on the SDN lists) to targeted restrictions (for those on the non-SDN lists).

Writing Company

The insurance entity that issues a policy. The name of the writing company will appear on the policy. Larger insurance companies may have multiple writing companies depending on the product and state or foreign jurisdiction where the policy is written.

INTRODUCTION TO ECONOMIC SANCTIONS

1
Introduction to Economic Sanctions

At its simplest, economic sanctions mean you are not allowed to do business with certain countries or parties. Before proceeding with a business transaction, you must do your homework to identify any potential sanctions issues.

This chapter will explain economic sanctions, their use, and which US government agency is in charge of implementing and enforcing them.

What Are Sanctions?

Sanctions are restrictions or penalties the government imposes on countries, people, groups, governments, or industries to help achieve certain goals in foreign policy and national security. For example, the United States may prohibit US citizens from engaging in particular trade or financial activities, or other dealings unless they get permission from OFAC or are expressly allowed to by law.[6] Since each sanctions program is based on different foreign policy and national security goals, prohibitions can vary from one program to another.[7]

Why Are Sanctions Used?

Sanctions are used instead of military force to change the behavior of individuals or governments. The goal is to alter their behavior without resorting to violence.

Specific reasons sanctions are imposed include:
- address human rights violations
- support democracy
- stop extremist groups by cutting off key resources needed to continue their activities
- protect national security interests
- protect international law
- preserve peace
- coerce a regime into changing its behavior or isolate the regime as a way of sending a broader political message internationally
- prevent conflicts and strengthen international security

What Countries Use Them?

Many countries have their own sanctions laws. Some examples include the US, the UK, Canada, Japan, and Australia. Even the European Union, which is comprised of many countries, has its own sanctions regime. Countries that are part of the EU must follow the sanctions set by the EU,[8] but they can also add their own prohibitions.

If your company does business in multiple countries—like selling to foreign customers, trading internationally, or working with foreign business partners—you might need to follow sanctions rules from several countries.

What Governmental Agency Is Responsible for Them?

The Office of Foreign Assets Control (OFAC), part of the US Department of the Treasury, oversees most US sanctions programs. OFAC enforces US sanctions laws civilly, while the Department of Justice handles criminal violations.

Some trade sanctions are managed by different agencies like the Department of State (DoS) and the Bureau of Industry and Security (BIS) of the Department of Commerce. These export control restrictions work alongside OFAC sanctions. They are essential for companies trading in exportable goods and will be discussed in more detail later in this guide.

2
How Economic Sanctions Are Created

Most sanctions programs are established and administered through Executive Orders, laws, and regulations.

Laws

US sanctions programs are based on laws passed by Congress. These laws give the President the emergency power to limit or prohibit international financial transactions, imports and exports, or entry into the US.[9]

Common laws cited to establish sanctions programs include the International Emergency Economic Powers Act (IEEPA), the Trading with the Enemy Act (TWEA), and the National Emergency Act (NEA). You don't need to know all the details of these laws to maintain an effective sanctions program, but it is important to understand they are what allow sanctions programs to exist.

Congress can also issue new sanctions directly via regulations. A couple of sanctions programs implemented in this matter include the Countering America's Adversaries Through Sanctions Act (CAATSA), which provides additional sanctions on Russia, Ukraine, Iran, and North Korea, and the Global Magnitsky Human Rights Accountability Act, covering global human rights abuses.

The law(s) on which a particular sanctions program is based are listed under "Statutes" on the program's page.

Executive Orders (EO)

When the President wants to impose new sanctions (under the authority of one of the previously mentioned laws), he will issue an Executive Order. The Executive Order explains why sanctions are needed, the laws under which the Executive Order is created (like TWEA), and who can be sanctioned under the program.

As an example, let's review the Executive Order for the Lebanon Sanctions Program.[10]

The Executive Order explains why sanctions are needed (in this instance, to protect democratic elections) and the laws under which the Executive Order is created (like IEEPA and the NEA).

Section 1 of the Executive Order describes who can be sanctioned under the program. In this case, people undermining Lebanon's democracy and parties providing them with financial or technical support. Section 1 also says that if someone is sanctioned, any assets they have in the US or with a US person get blocked. It also prohibits attempts to evade these sanctions.

You typically don't need to determine if the people you are doing business with fall into these categories. This Executive Order sets up a list-based program, so when someone is sanctioned under this program, they'll be added to the OFAC Specially Designated Nationals (SDN) list. You can check there. In a later chapter, you'll learn more about list-based sanctions and the SDN list.

These Executive Orders usually have other clauses, too. For instance, they might say that no one needs to be told beforehand they will be sanctioned, and the Department of Treasury (i.e., OFAC) can do whatever is required to carry out the order.

As time passes, more Executive Orders might get added to a program, expanding the scope of activity and parties that can be sanctioned. For example, the Russian Harmful Foreign Activities program has grown to include six Executive Orders. These orders prohibit additional activities like importing certain products from Russia into the US or investing in certain parts of the Russian economy.[11]

Regulations

OFAC will incorporate the sanctions laws and Executive Orders into its own regulations for a program, which are issued in the Code of Federal Regulations (CFR). The CFR is where all rules implemented by the Federal government are published.

For example, the Lebanese Program is codified at 31 CFR Part 549 Lebanon Sanction Regulations.[12]

Some programs operate only via Executive Order and do not have regulations published. For example, the Afghanistan program does not have OFAC-related regulations issued for it.[13]

It is essential to familiarize yourself with the CFR regulations to understand what's allowed and what's not under the program. However, not all information you need to comply with the program will be in the CFR regulations. Later, I'll discuss other helpful resources, such as guidance, general licenses, and frequently asked questions (FAQs) specific to a program but not part of the CFR.

Sanctions Programs

OFAC administers sanctions programs that consist of all the laws, Executive Orders, OFAC regulations, guidance, licenses, and FAQs related to restrictions against a specific country or activity. Some programs target activities in certain countries, such as Cuba, while some target specific activities globally, such as narcotics trafficking and weapons proliferation.

A country-based program does not mean that only people in that country are sanctioned. Parties anywhere in the world can be sanctioned under any program, including persons in the US and those in your country. For example, the Russian Harmful Foreign Activities Program imposes sanctions against individuals and entities anywhere in the world involved in specified harmful foreign activities of the Russian Federation.[14]

Also, programs may not exist indefinitely. For example, Sudan used to have a trade embargo, but it was discontinued several years ago, and Sudan is currently subject to only minimal sanctions.

The best place to find all of these documents is under the specific program's page on the OFAC website, the link for which is provided under References.

3

Who Has To Comply with Economic Sanctions?

Who must comply with economic sanctions? The answer is simple—everyone, including you! OFAC's definition of a US person is broad and can extend to individuals and businesses outside the US in certain situations.

You are required to comply with US sanctions if one of the following conditions exist:
- You are covered under the definition of a US Person.
- You are conducting a transaction with a US nexus.
- You are conducting activity covered by OFAC's secondary sanctions.

Who Is a Covered US Person?

You are a US Person and are covered by US sanctions in the following situations:

- US citizens anywhere in the world
- US-incorporated businesses, including their foreign branches
- people in the US for any reason, even if they are citizens of another country
- any party using the US financial system, US dollars, or US goods[15]

This means a foreign bank without US branches must also follow OFAC rules if it uses US dollars or the US financial system for a transaction.

For employees of global companies, it is crucial to know if your foreign entity is organized as a branch or subsidiary of the US-based entity. If it is a branch, it must always follow OFAC rules. If it is a subsidiary, it is not subject to OFAC regulations in most instances. However, it must comply with OFAC for business related to Iran, Cuba, and sometimes Russia and North Korea. This will be discussed further later in the chapter.

Who Else May Have To Comply?

There are situations where foreign parties may need to comply with US sanctions.

US-Nexus Transactions

US-nexus transactions occur when a transaction has a connection to the US. Here are some examples of transactions a foreign company can conduct with a US nexus (this is not a complete list of possibilities):

- conducting transactions through a US-based branch or subsidiary
- providing insurance that covers activity in the US
- a foreign subsidiary of a US insurance company providing coverage to a customer with property in Iran
- conducting a transaction where a US person is involved in any way
- purchasing or insuring goods that are of US origin or contain US-origin parts
- doing business through a US financial institution or a foreign branch of a US financial institution
- making or receiving a payment using US dollars
- transporting US-origin goods anywhere in the world

Correspondent banking is another way foreign companies and banks can unknowingly connect their transactions to the US, leading to sanctions violations. In correspondent banking, a US financial institution acts as a middleman for a foreign bank, allowing it to access the US banking system through a single account. All the transactions from the foreign bank's customers go through this one account. All transactions that flow through this account must comply with OFAC.

For example, Swedbank Latvia, a foreign bank subsidiary, was fined by OFAC for hundreds of transactions that violated sanctions on Crimea. A customer used Swedbank Latvia's online banking platform from a sanctioned jurisdiction to send payments to others also located in a sanctioned jurisdiction through Swedbank's US correspondent banks.[16]

Another way to have a US nexus is through omnibus accounts. Omnibus accounts are held with brokers and function like correspondent accounts, where one account combines all of a customer's assets and trades managed by a custodian. If your company uses omnibus accounts or trades through an omnibus account with a broker considered a US person, this creates a US nexus, which can lead to an OFAC violation.

In several instances, OFAC has fined foreign companies for not following OFAC rules while using the US financial system. For example, Toll Holdings, based in Australia, was fined by OFAC for routing payments through US financial institutions for shipments to or through comprehensively sanctioned countries or involving SDNs.[17]

Secondary Sanctions

Some US sanctions go beyond US borders (i.e., have "extraterritorial reach"). These are secondary sanctions.

Secondary sanctions are penalties imposed by one country on individuals, entities, or governments in another country for engaging in activities that violate the first country's sanctions or policies.[18] This means OFAC can require foreign parties not considered US persons to follow its rules or face getting sanctioned themselves. Usually, the punishment is getting shut out of the US financial system. Iran, North Korea, and Russia are examples of programs with secondary sanctions.

Here are a couple of examples of how this has worked recently:

- In 2018, the US left the Joint Comprehensive Plan of Action (JCPOA) agreement, which loosened sanctions on Iran in exchange for restrictions on Iran's nuclear program. After leaving the JCPOA, the US reinstated sanctions on Iran, including secondary sanctions for non-US parties trading with Iran in areas like energy, precious metals, finance, and software.[19]
- In late 2023, the US issued a new Executive Order 14114 for Russia.[20] It requires foreign financial institutions (FFIs) to comply with certain US sanctions against Russia. Specifically, FFIs can't do transactions for a sanctioned party in sectors of the Russian economy such as technology, defense, aerospace, and manufacturing. Nor can they conduct any transaction or provide any service or good to Russia's military. OFAC defined foreign financial institutions as banks, insurance companies, broker-dealers, and a host of other entities. So, a foreign bank not otherwise subject to OFAC's Russian-related sanctions would be subject to these regulations as an FFI.

Foreign companies must know what activity violates OFAC's secondary sanctions to avoid being shut out of the US financial system. With secondary sanctions, a foreign entity's transactions do not have to have a US nexus to be considered a violation by OFAC. It just has to violate the activity under which OFAC has implemented prohibitions.

For example, in May 2021, several Russian parties involved in constructing the Nord Stream 2 pipeline to Germany were sanctioned, none of whom were US persons.

In another instance, the US imposed secondary sanctions on Syrian businessmen for entering into otherwise legal contracts with the Syrian government without a US nexus. The US claimed they were "knowingly providing significant financial, material, or technological support to, or knowingly engaging in a significant transaction with, the Government of Syria."[21]

Foreign Subsidiaries of US Entities

I previously mentioned that foreign subsidiaries do not generally fall under the definition of a US person who must comply with US sanctions because OFAC defines a US person as a business incorporated in the United States and its foreign branches. However, as noted above, they may be subject to some secondary sanctions OFAC imposes on foreign entities. In addition, the Iran, North Korea, and Cuba sanctions programs have expanded the meaning of a US person to include foreign subsidiaries. I am including how each program includes foreign subsidiaries in its prohibitions.

- Cuba - The Cuban regulation defines "persons subject to the jurisdiction of the United States,"[22] which, in short, includes any entity, wherever organized or doing business, owned or controlled by a US person. This would cover foreign subsidiaries.
- Iran - Iranian regulations prohibit "an entity owned or controlled by a US person, set up outside the US," from dealing with Iran's government or citizens if that activity would be prohibited when conducted by a US person.[23] Again, this definition includes foreign subsidiaries.
- North Korea – North Korean regulations prohibit "a person owned or controlled by a US financial institution and established or maintained outside the United States" from conducting transactions with the Government of North Korea or a party sanctioned under North Korean

regulations.[24] This definition would include foreign subsidiaries of US financial institutions.

So, if your foreign company is a subsidiary of a US company and you sometimes do business in Cuba, Iran, or North Korea, you might get a warning from your sanctions compliance team not to conduct that business. If you ignore the warning, your company could face penalties from OFAC.

4
Types of Economic Sanctions

The term "sanctions" covers a wide range of actions the United States can take against a country, government, person, group, or industry, depending on what activity the US wants to stop. Generally, sanctions fall into three main categories: list-based sanctions, comprehensive country sanctions, and sectoral or trade sanctions.[25] Let's take a closer look at each one.

Comprehensive

Comprehensive sanctions, also known as trade embargoes, apply to a whole country. They restrict almost all commercial and financial activities involving the sanctioned country, including its government, individuals, businesses, and anyone acting on behalf of that country.[26]

Cuba, Iran, Syria, North Korea, and certain areas of Ukraine under Russian control, such as Crimea, face comprehensive sanctions from the US.

Even with comprehensive sanctions, some business activities are still allowed in these countries. We'll explore this further in a later chapter.

List-Based

OFAC uses different types of watchlists to enforce sanctions, with sanctioned parties placed on either the Specially Designated Nationals (SDN) watchlist, which carries full blocking prohibitions, or a Non-SDN watchlist, which has more targeted restrictions. Each list serves a different purpose, so if you find a customer is sanctioned, it's essential to know which list they're on and what specific restrictions apply. A wide range of parties can end up on the SDN list, including individuals, companies, groups, ships, aircraft, and even cryptocurrency wallets. A party can also appear on more than one watchlist. Let's dive into these lists in more detail.

The Specially Designated Nationals (SDN) List

When a party is sanctioned under an OFAC blocking program, they are added to the **"Specially Designated Nationals" (SDN)** list. Parties on the SDN list will face penalties like asset freezes, travel limits, import/export restrictions, and financial bans.[27] You also cannot do business with them.

These penalties deprive the SDN of economic resources they can use to further the activity the US wants to prevent. In a later chapter, we'll go into more detail on what to do if a customer is on the SDN list.

One example of a blocking program is the Global Magnitsky Sanctions Regulations.[28] The "Prohibited Transactions" section of these regulations states that "all property and interests in property... are blocked," which means you must stop all business with any party listed under this program.[29]

Non-SDN Lists

Parties on **Non-SDN Lists** are not SDNs and are not subject to full blocking prohibitions like those on the SDN list. Instead, they are subject to specific penalties, including export controls, import bans, financial transaction restrictions, and sectoral sanctions (i.e., restrictions on particular industries).

There are several non-SDN lists with different purposes, including:[30]

Sectoral Sanctions Identifications (SSI) List

This list focuses on certain sectors of the economy and specific parties operating in those industries. It is used primarily in the Ukraine-/Russia-related Sanctions program.[31] Restrictions are set through official orders called "Directives" and cover a wide range of restrictions.

A Directive is a determination issued by the President that certain activity is prohibited under an Executive Order. There might be limits on debt or equity, import/export restrictions, or restrictions on specific sectors such as energy, defense, and finance. For instance, if an entity is sanctioned under Directive 1, US persons are not allowed to engage in transactions involving new debt with a maturity longer than fourteen days or new equity of this entity.[32] Even though the SSI restricts certain activities by targeted parties, other dealings with these entities are still allowed, and their assets aren't frozen.

Non-SDN Menu-Based Sanctions List (NS-MBS List)

Parties on this list are not SDNs and are not covered by full blocking sanctions. Each party on the list can have different prohibitions. Their assets aren't blocked, but they face trade or financial restrictions, like restrictions on receiving certain goods or services and prohibitions on importing goods.[33]

For example, under the Counter Narcotics Trafficking Sanctions program, parties sanctioned under Executive Order 14059 may be restricted from receiving loans or credit, among other prohibitions.[34]

Non-SDN Chinese Military-Industrial Complex Companies List (NS-CMIC List)

These are Chinese companies that OFAC has determined have Chinese military ties. Again, they are not subject to full blocking sanctions. Instead, OFAC prohibits investment in these companies (i.e., purchasing their debt or equity such as stocks, bonds, or the mutual funds that invest in them).

Sectoral or Trade Sanctions

Sectoral or trade sanctions are the most complicated category to comply with. They prohibit specific activity with targeted entities in specified industries, while any other activity is legal. These sanctions may also ban some goods from being exported to or imported from the sanctioned country. The purpose is to weaken the country economically by targeting its most significant industries, thereby pushing it to end its unwanted behavior.

By definition, comprehensively sanctioned countries have trade sanctions. Sectoral sanctions, as discussed in the prior section, target certain sectors of the economy and specific parties operating in them. Trade sanctions, on the other hand, restrict imports and exports of goods and services to and from a sanctioned country. Let's discuss these types of trade sanctions and how they are used, using Russia as an example.

Targeting Industries

In Russia, sectoral sanctions impact significant industries, such as energy, financial, and minerals and mining, among others. Entities operating in these sectors in Russia can be hit with either blocking sanctions or non-SDN prohibitions.

For example, on September 15, 2022, OFAC authorized sanctions on individuals and entities operating in the quantum computing sector of Russia.[35]

Targeting Services

US persons are prohibited from providing certain services to parties in Russia, such as quantum computing, architecture, engineering, accounting, trust and corporate formation, and management consulting services.[36] US persons who do business in these sectors in Russia can be sanctioned. These prohibitions are established via Determinations, which are orders issued once it has been determined that a specific activity is prohibited under a previously issued Executive Order (E.O.).

For example, on September 15, 2022, OFAC issued a Determination under E.O. 14071 that USK persons cannot provide quantum computing services to anyone in Russia.[37] This service prohibition works in tandem with the related sectoral sanction targeting the industry to basically shut off any quantum computing-related activities in Russia.

However, the restrictions do not prohibit US persons from providing other services not covered by these sanctions.[38]

Some countries, like the UK and EU, may have different service prohibitions.

Targeting Import/Exports

Trade sanctions can prohibit the import of certain Russian goods into the US, such as fish and seafood, alcohol, and diamonds;[39] oil and petroleum products;[40] and Russian-origin aluminum, copper, and nickel,[41] among other items.

In coordination with OFAC, the Bureau of Industry and Security (BIS) and the Department of State (DoS) have restricted the export of many US-origin items to Russia, including electronics, mechanical components, technical components, manufacturing equipment, machine tools, and parts that can be used in Russia's military systems.[42]

Foreign companies doing business in countries facing OFAC import/export restrictions must ensure that their products are not US-origin or do not contain US-origin parts, as we'll discuss further in a later chapter.

Again, sectoral and trade sanctions do not ban US persons from all transactions with targeted companies—only those involving restricted activities or goods.

Sanctioned Parties Not on Any List

The most challenging part of complying with sanctions is when parties are considered sanctioned despite not appearing on any SDN or Non-SDN list. This can occur in a couple of ways.

First, some OFAC sanctions block categories of persons even if they do not appear on the SDN List.[43] For example, for the Venezuelan sanctions program, Executive Order 13884 blocks any person who meets the definition of the "Government of Venezuela."[44] Also, OFAC's Cuba sanctions prohibit most transactions with Cuban nationals.[45]

The second way is commonly called the "50 Percent Rule."[46] This rule kicks in when a company is majority-owned (50 percent or more) by one or more sanctioned parties. This includes both direct and indirect ownership. These entities are considered sanctioned even if they aren't on the SDN list.

No official government list of companies owned by sanctioned parties exists, but some private companies, like Dow Jones, create and maintain such lists.

Let's look at an example of how this works. Goode Company has three owners: Bad Co., which is on the SDN list, owns 30 percent of the company; Worst Inc., which is also on the SDN list, owns 25 percent of the company; Best LLC, which is not on the SDN list, owns the remaining 45 percent. Because two of the owners of Goode Company are SDNs, and together they own 55 percent of the company (a majority), Good Company is also considered an SDN, even though it is not on the SDN list.

Note that Best LLC is not sanctioned, despite being an owner of Goode Company and a partner with Bad Co. and Worst Inc. Just because a branch or subsidiary is sanctioned does not automatically make a parent company sanctioned.

The example above dealt with direct ownership. This gets more complicated when indirect ownership is involved.

Let's use the Goode Company example again.

Goode Company has three owners: Bad Co. owns 30 percent, Worst Inc. owns 25 percent, and Best LLC owns 45 percent. None of these three entities are on an SDN list. However, Bad Co. and Worst Inc. are both 50 percent owned by Sanctioned Person A, so both are deemed sanctioned. Therefore, with 55 percent ownership by sanctioned parties, Goode Company is also considered sanctioned due to its majority indirect ownership by Sanctioned Person A.

When parties are sanctioned, they frequently divest part of their ownership in entities where they are the majority owners so that the entities are not deemed sanctioned. For example, to avoid being blocked by Russian sanctions, some majority owners of Russian companies, like Rusal, divested part or all of their ownership to fall just below the 50 percent mark.[47]

The US's 50 Percent Rule functions differently from the UK's and the EU's 50 Percent Rule, which will be discussed in a later chapter.

5
How Economic Sanctions Affect Your Job and Your Company

Economic sanctions impact your entire organization—every employee, every department, and every business line—especially in global industries. So, your organization is likely affected.

While compliance professionals are directly impacted, the need to be knowledgeable about and comply with sanctions does not end with them. Employees handling tasks with a sanctions nexus must also understand and adhere to sanctions requirements.

This list isn't exhaustive, but it highlights key roles that may have a sanctions nexus that will need sanctions procedures and training within your organization:

- payment processors (such as a payment for goods or services, claim, refund, or vendor payment)
- originate a payment on an account
- open new accounts
- underwrite policies or loans
- conduct customer due diligence
- import or export goods
- conduct marine shipments
- contract with vendors or other business partners
- sell products or services
- hire staff
- claims adjustors
- product development
- legal/compliance
- customer service

If you are self-employed and sell things or provide services, it affects you as an individual, too.

Let's look at a few examples of how the jobs listed above can encounter sanctions issues:

- Accounts Receivable (AR): AR invoices customers and receives payments. If AR invoices Joe Designee but receives a payment from Jane Designee, both Joe and Jane must be scanned against OFAC's lists to ensure they aren't sanctioned parties. AR staff may need to scan names manually before invoicing and prior to posting payments unless an automated system handles this. At a minimum, AR staff should understand that OFAC rules apply to their jobs so they can respond appropriately if compliance needs extra information or funds need to be blocked.

- Sales: Teams who handle product sales need to understand sanctions regulations to avoid selling to sanctioned parties or shipping restricted goods to sanctioned countries, especially US-origin products. They should be cautious to avoid any actions leading to illegal transaction structuring, sanctions evasion, facilitating illicit transactions, or indirect sales to sanctioned parties.
- Human Resources (HR): HR should scan all potential hires to ensure they are not sanctioned before onboarding. This includes employees hired through outside staffing firms and temporary employees. HR must ensure that both the staffing firm and the employees they provide are not sanctioned.
- Payment Processing: Processors handle payments made to accountholders who request withdrawals. All payees must be scanned before the payment goes out the door, especially if the payment is going via wire, which is immediately sent. In addition, if the payment is destined for a foreign country, you must verify that it is not a comprehensively sanctioned country and that the payment is not otherwise prohibited, such as being sent to an account at a sanctioned bank.
- Shipping: The shipping department must be aware of sanctions and know how to identify any issues involving OFAC, such as shipments containing US-origin goods or involving US entities (e.g., a US-based shipping company). They should gather necessary shipment details and know when to flag shipments for sanctions review. For instance, if a US-origin product is being shipped to Russia, they should ensure it's reviewed to confirm it's not a prohibited item or going to a sanctioned party.
- Claims Adjusting: Claims adjusters review claims and issue payments. Before any payment is issued, all payees must be checked

against sanctions lists. For payments going to foreign countries, they need to confirm the country is not comprehensively sanctioned and that the payment isn't going to a sanctioned bank. Adjusters must understand sanctions well, as there are many ways a claim can have an OFAC nexus through the goods involved, involved parties (like vendors), or connections to the US financial system. A claim with a US nexus could cause compliance issues if an adjuster doesn't identify it and refer it for a sanctions review.
- Underwriting: Underwriters evaluate insurance applications and determine coverage. Before issuing a policy, all included parties—such as the primary insured, additional insureds, contractors, and counterparties—must be screened against sanctions watchlists. Underwriters should also be able to identify other sanctions risks, like coverage in sanctioned countries and whether a sanctions nexus in a new policy may affect issuance, and know to refer those issues to sanctions compliance for review.

If you think about it, there are few jobs within a company without a sanctions nexus. So it's vital that all employees are trained in sanctions generally and your organization has procedures for these employees to follow.

Now that you have a solid grasp of how sanctions work, it's time to focus on preventing violations within your company. The next section kicks off with the most crucial step—building a strong economic sanctions compliance program.

SETTING UP AN ECONOMIC SANCTIONS COMPLIANCE PROGRAM (SCP)

6
How Do I Comply with Economic Sanctions?

OFAC prohibits all parties subject to US sanctions from doing business with sanctioned parties. How you follow that requirement is up to you.

Start by setting up a basic sanctions compliance program that outlines how you will comply with regulations. If you already have a program, compare it to OFAC's recommendations to identify necessary improvements.[48]

Establish a Sanctions Program

A sanctions compliance program (SCP) is comprised of the policies, procedures, and controls that help a company follow sanctions regulations. Depending on your company's size and whether it operates worldwide or just in the United States, your program might include some or all of these elements. In subsequent chapters, we'll go into more detail about each component.

At a minimum, a company should have a sanctions compliance program that encompasses:

- a Sanctions Compliance Officer (SCO) or other responsible party–Chapter 7
- an economic sanctions policy–Chapter 8
- a risk assessment–Chapter 16
- written procedures–Chapter 9
- internal controls–Chapters 10, 11, and 24
- contract language–Chapter 12
- environmental scanning–Chapter 13
- training–Chapter 14
- auditing and testing–Chapter 15

The Plain-English Guide to Developing an Economic Sanctions Program Workbook can assist you in developing your program with easy-to-use worksheets that cover every step in the process.

Let's discuss these key sections of an SCP in more detail.

7
Sanctions Compliance Officer/Responsible Party

Someone within the company should be responsible for overseeing the SCP. This includes oversight for all aspects of the program, direct supervision of the sanctions compliance team if there is one, and indirect oversight of any additional staff performing sanctions-related duties.

In larger companies, the person may be called the sanctions compliance officer (SCO). OFAC does not require a company to appoint an SCO but recommends it in its compliance guidance.[49] In larger companies, it is a good idea for someone to hold this title so that employees know who to contact with sanctions questions. Alternatively, these duties may rest with the chief compliance officer (CCO), chief risk officer (CRO), or chief legal officer (CLO), who may have other responsibilities in addition to sanctions compliance.

The SCO should have enough independence and authority to act within the company. Ideally, this should be someone at the management level or higher. The person should be allowed to take necessary actions to address any issues with the sanctions program. They should have direct access to senior management without going through several other management layers. Periodic meetings with senior management should occur to provide updates on the status of the sanctions program.

The sanctions function overseen by the SCO may be a stand-alone group (referred to as the "sanctions compliance team" or just "sanctions compliance") or part of a larger group, such as financial crimes or the anti-money laundering team. The sanctions function may also include staff in other departments whose jobs have a sanctions nexus (such as accounts payable).

Some responsibilities of the sanctions compliance officer include:
- maintaining and updating the economic sanctions policy
- developing procedures
- conducting the risk assessment
- overseeing staff who perform sanctions-related procedures
- administering sanctions training

- working with other teams within the company to implement sanctions controls
- updating senior management on sanctions issues and projects
- acting as a liaison with external legal counsel
- filing required reports with OFAC

The SCO should also have enough resources to do their job effectively. This includes having the correct number of staff with the necessary expertise and access to technology, training, and other resources to adequately manage sanctions compliance.

8
Economic Sanctions Policy

The cornerstone of the SCP is an economic sanctions policy. The policy will outline your company's commitment to sanctions compliance and briefly describe the procedures and controls for compliance.

Key best practices when drafting or updating your sanctions policy:
- It should be risk-based and tailored to your company's specific risks.
- It should be written in plain, easy-to-read language since everyone in the company must be familiar with it.
- If employees are located in foreign countries, it should be translated into their native language.
- It should be reviewed and updated annually or whenever significant updates are made to sanctions regulations or your program.
- It should be stored in an area (such as an online shared site) where all staff can review it.

Sections to include in your policy:
- senior management's commitment to fostering a culture of compliance
- pertinent definitions for key terms such as sanctions, sanctioned parties, prohibited transactions, etc.
- sanctions laws applicable to your company, both domestic and foreign
- potential penalties to the company and the individual for non-compliance
- who the policy applies to in the company and whether third parties such as vendors and business partners must comply with your policy
- the person responsible for the program and their duties
- that a risk assessment is conducted
- high-level description of internal controls
- who will receive sanctions training
- testing and auditing of the program
- methods to report potential violations

These sections are discussed in more detail below.

Senior Management Commitment

OFAC believes senior management's commitment and support for an organization's SCP are crucial factors in determining its success.[50] Senior management's commitment also demonstrates to the rest of the company that sanctions compliance is a priority for the firm's success.

Your policy should clearly state that senior management is committed to sanctions compliance and will not conduct business that violates sanctions.

Unfortunately, there have been many cases where companies, despite having what seemed like robust sanctions compliance programs, received hefty fines from OFAC. This occurs when senior management merely pays lip service to compliance and undermines controls to carry out transactions that breach sanctions or aid sanctioned parties and countries.

Some considerations that will demonstrate senior management commitment to OFAC:[51]

- Sanctions compliance should be part of an overall "culture of compliance" within your company. This means your company and its senior management are dedicated to ethics and compliance in all business dealings, not just sanctions. If your company has a Code of Ethics, sanctions should be included.
- Senior management should review and approve the sanctions compliance policy.
- The sanctions compliance function should receive adequate resources, such as the appropriate number of staff with sufficient expertise, technology, training, and other resources to support compliance.
- The sanctions compliance function should have sufficient authority and autonomy within the company. This means the person appointed to oversee sanctions compliance should be at a level within the company that allows them to work independently and take any appropriate actions to address issues with the sanctions program.
- Senior management should be involved when potential regulatory violations occur or material deficiencies are identified in the program. They should also approve how gaps or issues are addressed and any OFAC filings.

Pertinent Definitions for Key Terms

Since your policy will need to be read and understood by all employees, even those who don't regularly work in positions that encounter sanctions issues, you should define key terms such as "sanctions," "sanctioned parties or Specially Designated Nationals (SDNs)," and "prohibited transactions" as well as any other technical terms that are in your policy. Reviewing the Definitions chapter at the beginning of this guide may be a good start.

Sanctions Laws Applicable to Your Company

This section should state what jurisdiction(s) your company is subject to. If you are solely a domestic company with no foreign customers, business partners, vendors, or sales, then you may only be subject to US sanctions (OFAC). If you do business globally, you may want to mention other jurisdictions you operate in regularly, such as Canada, the United Kingdom (UK), or the European Union (EU), as your company will need to comply with sanctions in those jurisdictions as well.

Potential Penalties for Non-Compliance

This section should briefly explain the penalties for sanctions violations to the company and the individual employee. The penalties should include potential monetary fines, job-related consequences such as termination, jail time, and negative media against the company.

Who the Policy Applies to

This paragraph should explain that the policy applies to everyone within the company, from line staff up to executives and the Board of Directors. You may also want it to apply to external parties, such as business partners, joint venture partners, vendors, contractors, etc. If you do, you will want to ensure these third parties know your policy and its expectations. My prior firm had a Vendor Code of Ethics that outlined our expectations for ethical behavior, including compliance with sanctions. Our vendors had to follow these policies.

Responsibilities

Your policy should clearly state that the SCO is responsible for the sanctions compliance program and might also list some of the key responsibilities.

Risk Assessment

This section will mention that your sanctions compliance program is based on risk and may briefly describe how risk is determined. A separate written procedure or an addendum to the policy may describe in detail how the risk assessment is conducted. Completing a risk assessment will be discussed in more detail in a later section.

Internal Controls

Internal controls are the processes, procedures, and measures that prevent and detect sanctions violations. Your policy may list high-level controls such as sanctions screening and exclusion language in contracts.

Training

Everyone in an organization likely needs basic sanctions knowledge and training. Some employees who encounter sanctions issues regularly may require more detailed training. You should describe in your sanctions policy who will receive sanctions training, how often it will be rolled out, how it will be tracked, and who will provide it.

Testing and Auditing

Your sanctions program should be reviewed and tested to identify any gaps in the program that may prevent it from operating effectively. This can be done through periodic compliance testing and auditing. The policy should indicate that testing and auditing will occur, who will conduct it, and the frequency. It's ok to specify the frequency as "periodically" or "at least once every three years."

Reporting Violations

Depending on your company's size, employees may have multiple ways to report inappropriate conduct. Some examples may include contacting a manager, calling an anonymous hotline, or escalating to the SCO or the CCO.

If you find drafting a policy daunting, many companies post their sanctions compliance policy online. You can find plenty of examples to get you started writing your own policy.

9

Written Sanctions Procedures

Any procedures supporting sanctions-related processes should be in writing. This shows OFAC, auditors, and internal parties like the CCO that procedures are in place and how they work, and it serves as a valuable training tool for new staff.

Here's a list of procedures you may consider implementing in your company. The specific procedures you choose will depend on your company's risk level, size, and scope of operations:

- how to review and clear alerts from a scanning application
- how and when to manually scan business
- when other departments need to refer business to the sanctions compliance team or SCO for review
- what steps to take if a customer is sanctioned
- how to conduct a risk assessment
- how to escalate sanctions issues (such as a potential violation)
- how and when to contact OFAC (filing blocked asset and rejected transaction reports, applying for specific licenses, filing a voluntary self-disclosure, etc.)

Best Practices for Procedures

Decide which processes need written procedures. Then, determine what staff members need to perform them. Do all of your sanctions procedures rest with the sanctions compliance team, or do employees in other departments also need written procedures for handling sanctions-related tasks? For example, if you have banking, treasury, or accounts receivable/accounts payable functions, they may need procedures for when to scan payees and payors manually. Other lines of business may need written guidelines on when to refer a transaction or piece of business to sanctions compliance for review. The CCO may also need to review and provide input on some of the procedures, such as those for escalating sanctions issues to senior management.

Collaborate on procedures with the people responsible for carrying them out. This lesson was hard-learned from my previous role. When you create procedures solely based on your vision, they may not be feasible for the staff tasked with implementing them, and they will push back on doing them or not do them at all. Engage with the team from the start; they often have valuable insights on executing the process effectively. This approach ensures their initial support for the procedure and increases the likelihood of its success.

Some additional best practices for written procedures:
- Even though several departments may handle the procedures, it's crucial to have one person, like the SCO, oversee all sanctions-related processes.
- Maintain the documents in a common area (for example, an online shared site) so the most recent version can be easily accessed.
- Procedures should be reviewed and updated at least annually or when there is a significant update to a process.
- You may want to maintain a list of all your procedures with their current version number and the date they were last revised.

How to Write a Procedure

If you've never written a procedure before, it can be daunting. Below are some suggested ways to go about drafting your process document:
- Clearly title the document. What does this document cover? For example, "When to Refer a Transaction to Sanctions Compliance." It's clear that staff should consult this document to determine if the business they are working on needs to be referred. Don't just title it "Referral Procedures," as that's vague. Refer to whom and for what?
- More critical procedures, especially those conducted by persons outside of the sanctions compliance team, may benefit from identifying the scope and purpose of the document. Why does this procedure exist, and who needs to follow it? For example, in the first bullet, the scope and purpose may be as follows: "This document will assist claims handlers in identifying when a claim needs to be referred to sanctions compliance for review before a payment is issued."
- A revision date and/or version number may be included so staff can quickly identify that they are using the most current version.

- Who is responsible for the procedure? If you have a scope and purpose, this is probably already listed. If not, you can note that here. For example, "the sanctions compliance team is responsible for this process."
- Go step-by-step. This document will help train new staff and remind current staff of the correct procedures. If you can walk through the process first, that would be best. Don't skip any steps, even if they seem obvious, to avoid confusing the reader. Use clear and concise language. Organize the steps logically. Some people may start by completing a high-level flowchart that shows how the process works.
- Use screenshots if the document explains how to use a system. For example, in a procedure detailing how to clear alerts in your sanctions screening system, include screenshots from your application. These could show where to find information, input clearing reasons, how to close alerts, and how to attach documents. It's much easier to show the appropriate tab to click with a screenshot rather than to describe how to find it in words.
- Remember to obtain input on the process from the people who will perform it and have them review it before you finalize it in case something is unclear or you missed a step.
- Once it's finalized, distribute it to all staff who will perform the procedure and their managers and post it on your shared internal site for easy access to updates. Some teams may have their own process manuals to which the new procedure needs to be added. Provide training, if necessary, on the new process.

10

Setting Up a Scanning Program

Most emphasis on complying with sanctions is on scanning, also known as screening. Scanning involves checking a party's name (customer, vendor, employee, payee, etc.) against sanctions watchlists to see if there is a match. Surprisingly, OFAC does not require anyone to scan their business. However, no compliance program would be effective without it. The best practice is establishing a written sanctions program documenting who, when, how, and how often you will conduct sanctions screening.

Scanning Program

The sanctions screening program should be in writing and consist of the following elements:
- what criteria an automated sanctions screening solution should include
- what sanctions watchlists to include in your scanning program
- what parties and transactions will be scanned
- what threshold(s) will be used to scan data
- how often data will be scanned
- when manual scanning should be conducted
- how potential matches will be cleared or escalated
- how to handle positive matches
- periodic testing of the application to ensure it's functioning as expected

Automated Scanning Application

The best way to implement a sanctions screening program is with an automated scanning application. Once it's set up correctly, it requires minimal effort to keep it running. Instead of relying solely on manual scanning—which is time-consuming and prone to mistakes—an automated system lets you focus on reviewing potential matches only rather than sorting through every transaction.

Some companies that offer sanctions screening applications include Lexis Nexis, Moody's, and Computer Services, Inc. (CSI).

When vetting a system, you should ask:
- What watchlists do you provide? Some companies offer hundreds of lists from around the world, including non-sanction lists like those excluding people from federally funded healthcare programs. This might be too much for your company. On the other hand, a smaller vendor might only provide US sanctions lists when you need global lists, too.
- Does the vendor keep the sanctions lists up-to-date, or do you? Most vendors will update the watchlists themselves. If you use lists in addition to the ones provided by the vendor, you may be required to keep those lists updated, which can be a hassle.
- How soon after a list is updated is your system updated? Same-day updating is ideal. OFAC has sanctioned companies for conducting transactions on behalf of a party sanctioned on the same day the transaction was made.[52]
- Do they use "fuzzy logic" to identify matches? Fuzzy logic means using variations in spelling, phonetics, and name transposition (switching of first and last names, for example) to determine a potential match.
- Can clearing logic be recorded in the system? Clearing logic is how you determine that a potential match is a false hit and not a positive match. It's important to record your reasons for clearing a match in the system, so you have proof if questions come up later.
- Can documents be attached in the system? If you use documents to clear a hit, you will want to attach that to the alert for future reference.
- Can you scan data against different watchlists and different thresholds depending on what the data is? Depending on your size and the data you want to scan, you may not want to screen all your data against the same watchlists at the same threshold. If you have international and domestic business, you may want to screen the domestic business only against US lists while screening international business against global lists.
- How long do you retain the alerts, clearing reasons, and attached documents? Data should be accessible for at least five years in case

you need to provide information to OFAC or auditors. Otherwise, ten years is a good guideline.
- Is there a whitelist or "good customer list" you can add people to? Once you clear a customer as a match to a sanctioned party, you don't want to look at that alert again. A whitelist or good customer list allows you to add these false positives to a list so that they won't alert again if rescanned unless they hit against a new sanctioned party.
- Is the system user-friendly? Is it easy to determine which of your customers is a potential match and to whom they are a match? Your customer can match to multiple people on the sanctions lists, and you'll need to be able to identify, review, and clear each one individually.
- Is it easy for your data files to be loaded and scanned through the system? It would be best to set up a process to automatically create and feed new data files into the screening application.

What Data Should Be Scanned?

Everyone you do business with should be scanned. This includes:
- all customers (including joint accountholders or multiple insureds under an insurance policy)
- beneficiaries of accounts
- payees to whom checks are issued
- payors who make a payment or deposit on an account
- employees
- vendors
- other business partners, such as attorneys
- third-party claimants (for example, under an auto policy or a loss adjustor)
- joint venture partners
- merger and acquisition targets
- counterparties of trades

If you ship goods, the list of participants who should be scanned is even longer, including:
- purchaser
- seller

- shipper
- shipping company
- vessel name
- consignee
- freight forwarder
- the ultimate beneficiary of the shipment
- countries the shipment is transiting
- goods shipped

If you sell high-risk or dual-use goods, you should screen them against their destination to ensure they are not prohibited from being exported there.

Finally, you should also scan countries you are doing business in to know they are not the target of a trade embargo.

OFAC considers an entire transaction prohibited if even one party to it is sanctioned.

How Do We Scan This Data?

If you have multiple systems with data (i.e., customers in one database, payments flowing through another), you'll need to figure out how to extract data from each system to feed through your sanctions screening application. Your IT person should be your initial contact for this task. They'll understand the data that can be extracted, how to do it, and how to format it into a file that can be uploaded and scanned into your sanctions screening application. Most systems allow uploads in Excel, comma-delimited text files, or similar formats.

Larger organizations can arrange real-time scanning by connecting their system, such as a payment system, to the sanctions screening application using an API (Application Protocol Interface). This connection instantly checks payee or customer names entered into the system against the sanctions screening application, giving immediate results (match or no match).

For situations where data cannot be automatically scanned or scanned promptly, manual scanning can be conducted. OFAC offers manual scanning of its lists through the OFAC website: https://sanctionssearch.ofac.treas.gov/. Our company set up an internal website with an API that let employees screen names against a select group of global watchlists. This helped staff quickly check wire payments or new business without sending it to sanctions compliance and waiting for a response, saving time for everyone.

How Often and When Should Data Be Scanned?

How often and when you scan your data depends on the level of risk involved. For example, a business selling jewelry online might only need to check a customer's name when processing payments. However, companies that manage accounts, like banks or insurers, should screen transactions as they happen and periodically rescan their entire customer list.

In general, OFAC will expect you to scan data **before**:
- onboarding a new customer
- issuing a policy
- sending a payment
- conducting a transaction
- receiving a payment and depositing it into your account
- signing a contract
- renewing a contract or policy
- shipping goods

For businesses managing accounts, periodic rescans are necessary, even if no transactions have occurred recently, as OFAC prohibits maintaining accounts, contracts, or policies with sanctioned parties.

This doesn't mean you need to screen your data daily. While OFAC updates its watchlists regularly, it's not a daily occurrence. However, OFAC requires that your watchlists stay up-to-date and that you rescan them immediately after any updates. Most automated systems will update your data within 24 hours of a watchlist change.

How often you run scans depends on risk. Some information, like new accounts or payments, should be scanned daily. Higher-risk records, such as those of foreign customers, should be rescanned daily or whenever the lists are updated. Lower-risk categories, like domestic vendors, can be checked monthly or at another appropriate interval.

Many automated screening systems maintain a customer database. This allows the system to automatically rescan all parties when sanctions lists (like those from the US or the UK) are updated. The database is built by storing every scanned item for ongoing monitoring.

This practice helps ensure compliance and protects your company from inadvertently working with sanctioned parties.

What Sanctions Lists Should We Use?

If you operate solely within the United States (no foreign customers, employees, or vendors), you can use OFAC's sanctions lists. However, OFAC has several watchlists: SDN lists (complete blocking prohibitions) and non-SDN lists (other targeted restrictions). Whenever your transaction has a US nexus, you should ensure your scanning system screens them all.

If you have any foreign business, customers, or business partners, you should include the foreign government sanctions watchlists for relevant countries. Most countries have their own lists, but you may not do business in all those countries. Some top picks are Canada, the UK, the EU, and Australia. A comprehensive global sanctions dataset is necessary for companies operating in multiple countries. Dow Jones offers a list that can be integrated into your screening solution as an additional watchlist.

If you deal in goods (buying, shipping, distributing, or insuring), you must also scan the BIS and DoS lists for parties prohibited from exporting US-origin goods. A consolidated list where you can manually scan all these lists at once is located here: https://www.trade.gov/consolidated-screening-list. Otherwise, most sanctions application vendors will include those lists in their datasets that are available for scanning.

What Threshold Should We Use?

A threshold is the level at which the sanctions screening application considers a party a potential match to a sanctioned party. For example, your customer "Jose C. Rodriguez" may match against "Jose Rodrigues" or "Jose P Rodriguez" at a 95 percent threshold.

The threshold you use will depend on your application testing, which is discussed later in this chapter. You probably won't want to set all of your thresholds to 100 percent (exact name matches), but you also don't want them set so low (such as 85 percent) that you get hundreds of false positives to sift through. Higher-risk data, such as foreign customers, should generally be scanned at a lower threshold to capture name variations. For example, Hispanic customers may have two last names (father's surname and mother's surname), which they may not use consistently. Asian customers might list their surname first and their given name second. A lower threshold will account for these variations (i.e., via "fuzzy logic").

How Should We Clear Potential Matches?

There are a lot of common names on the OFAC lists, so you will likely find a customer who is a name match. . For example, the name "Jose Rodriguez" will produce nine hits at a 100 percent threshold. Are any of these hits positive matches?

Matches are usually determined to be a "false positive" (i.e., not an actual match) after comparing your customer information to the information on the SDN provided by OFAC. Obtain information from your customer, such as middle name, Social Security Number, Date of Birth, and address history, that you can compare to the party on the SDN list to clear this potential match.

Define what criteria you will use to clear an alert. For example, do you rely solely on name, address, and date of birth, or can you use a customer's social media profile picture to estimate their age compared to the sanctioned party? Additionally, specify how many criteria must match to deem it a positive match—name only, name and address, name and date of birth, or all three?

Remember, people move, so not having a match on the address is usually insufficient to clear an alert. You may want to review their address history (obtained from the customer or a public records search such as Lexis Nexis) to verify how long they've lived at certain addresses and whether they've ever lived in the same state or country as the sanctioned party.

I don't recommend using photos to clear an alert, as you don't know how old the images are. Use self-reported information, such as on Facebook or LinkedIn, sparingly and only if you can verify it is your customer's profile, not someone of the same name.

You can also search for information on public sites like occupational licenses, home ownership, and property tax records to find information on your customer that can help clear a false positive. News articles showing your sanctioned party operating in a different occupation in a different country from your customer can also help clear a potential match.

If you struggle to clear a match, contact OFAC for guidance. OFAC prefers companies not report matches unless they are confident it's positive. If your customer's information doesn't agree with the SDN details, it's probably safe to clear the alert as a false positive.

The good news for foreign companies is that if you have an OFAC match but, after review, you have no US nexus, then it's likely not business you have to reject or terminate.

However, if it is a match, a later chapter covers what OFAC expects you to do next.

Do I Need to Document This?

Yes, keep records of how you confirmed someone isn't a match to the SDN. You might need this information if they show up again as a match or you are asked about it. In my prior role, banks often asked about customers we initiated transactions for who popped up on their sanctions check system. Most automated scanning applications will have space to document your clearing reasons and attach documentation.

Written Procedures for Sanctions Screening

Written procedures about the sanctions screening process should include:
- How the sanctions compliance team will review and clear potential alerts generated by the system. Your procedures should outline the criteria for clearing an alert and specify how many criteria must match to deem it a positive match.
- When a potential match should be escalated to the sanctions compliance officer for review.
- How positive matches are handled, including rejecting transactions, blocking assets, or dissolving the business relationship.
- How positive matches, rejected transactions, blocked property, and possible violations are reported to OFAC.
- When other staff within the company should refer a transaction or account to sanctions compliance for review.

You may want to document (a spreadsheet will do) what data is scanned, what internal system the data is from, what watchlists and thresholds are used, how frequently the data is screened, and your reasoning for these parameters. This will help track that you are scanning all necessary data and assist in the risk assessment.

Periodic Testing of the Application

It's important to occasionally test your scanning application to ensure it's working as expected. Vendors often update their scanning engines, especially their fuzzy logic, which can affect the quality of alerts over time. Your vendor likely has a test environment for the screening application that you can use and won't incur scanning charges.

When to Test
- Test the system when it's first set up.
- Test periodically based on risk, but at least once every three to five years.
- Test when there are significant changes in your company's operations, like acquiring a foreign entity with higher-risk business.

How to Test
- Feed test data through your application to see what alerts appear at different threshold levels.
- Use sanctioned party data from various OFAC and global watchlists.
- Adjust entries (transpose names, misspell names, change residence countries, etc.) and scan them at different thresholds (such as 90 percent, 95 percent, and 99 percent).
- Evaluate the alerts at each threshold, looking for quality alerts you'd expect to review, not just positive matches. Also, look for alerts you expected to receive but did not.
- Scan current "live" data files (i.e., actual business data) at the same thresholds and watchlists to compare results. This will help you calibrate the system for your business.

Evaluate Results
- Determine if any watchlists must be changed based on the test results.
- Find the threshold(s) for each watchlist that provides the best mix of quality alerts and minimal false positives. Avoid using a threshold that

generates mostly false positives just to catch a rare misspelled sanctioned party name.

Documentation

Document your testing process, results, changes made, and approvals received. This ensures you have a record of your methods and decisions, which is crucial for compliance and future reference.

Referral Process

However, you cannot rely on scanning alone. Your automated system may not identify all sanctions risks for a transaction.

For instance, let's say you have a product liability insurance policy for a US-based customer. The policy documents reveal that they sell their products in Russia, China, and Cuba. While your system will scan the customer and related parties covered by the policy, it may not be able to capture, feed, and screen all countries covered.

In another example, your customer in the UK has a US bank as a counterparty, and the transaction involves sending goods to Cuba. That data may not appear in your administrative system and may not be sent to your screening application.

Or, an insurance claim occurs in Iranian waters, but your screening system only receives data that shows the customer, the claimant, and the vendors involved in the loss are all non-sanctioned.

That is why a referral process is so important!

Our automated system couldn't catch all the sanctions risks in the policies we wrote, so we set up a referral process for underwriters and claims handlers. For higher-risk policies and claims, we created a straightforward procedure for when and how they should refer cases to the sanctions compliance team. We also trained them on this process and explained why it's crucial. Employee referrals and automated screening are essential to a company's sanctions screening program.

What transactions should you include in your referral program? Consider any risks linked to comprehensively sanctioned countries or higher-risk nations like Russia and Venezuela, where US sanctions differ from other countries' sanctions. Staff will need a clear understanding of what constitutes a sanctions nexus. For the above examples, the underwriter of the product liability policy would refer the business as the customer wants to cover Cuban sales, the employee setting up the Cuban transaction would refer the business as there is a US bank counterparty, and the claims adjuster would refer the claim as it occurred in Iranian waters.

Final Thoughts on Scanning

While an automated scanning process goes a long way toward ensuring sanctions compliance, remember that scanning cannot be your only control. At my prior organization, staff thought that if customer names were being scanned, we complied with OFAC regulations. That is not the case. Scanning won't catch everything.

Not all transaction details needing review may pass through your sanctions screening program. As a result, certain sanctions risks might be overlooked. In such cases, the transaction should be referred to the SCO or sanctions compliance team for manual review to ensure compliance with trade embargoes and OFAC regulations. This underscores the importance of having both automated scanning and manual referral processes.

11
Due Diligence

A company should do two types of checks to spot possible sanctions problems before moving forward with business: one for its customers and another for its third-party business partners.

Customer Due Diligence

Customer due diligence means getting to know your customers to understand their risks. This includes the following procedures:
- checking a customer's name against sanctions watchlists
- finding out who owns and runs the customer's business (beneficial ownership)
- scanning beneficial owners' names against sanctions watchlists
- looking for any sanctions-related red flags in their business activities (such as geographic location)
- searching for any negative news about the customer, like past sanctions fines or if they have connections to sanctioned parties

If your company has an Anti-Money Laundering Program, it likely already has customer due diligence procedures, including a sanctions check you can leverage.

Next, we'll explore two key challenges in customer due diligence.

Legal Entities and Ultimate Beneficial Ownership (UBO)

Various legal entities like LLCs, LPs, LLPs, and PLCs are commonly used by sanctioned parties to conceal their assets. These entities often obscure ownership details, especially when incorporated in jurisdictions like Jersey or the Cayman Islands with opaque registration rules. Sanctioned individuals may further complicate matters by structuring these entities to be owned by other entities, making uncovering true ownership challenging. Some companies, such as Dow Jones and Lexis Nexis, have compiled databases of the ultimate beneficial owner of various legal entities. In addition, entities are now required to file beneficial ownership information with FinCEN under the Beneficial Ownership Information Reporting Rule.[53]

However, these databases aren't infallible. When dealing with customers operating under one of these legal entities, requesting information and documentation of ultimate beneficial ownership during customer due diligence is essential to ensure compliance and avoid engaging with sanctioned parties. Russian oligarchs, in particular, use these vehicles to hide assets, ownership, and control of their businesses.

Politically Exposed Persons (PEPs)

Politically Exposed Persons (PEPs) add another layer of complexity to customer due diligence. A PEP is someone who holds a high-ranking public position in a domestic or foreign government—this includes presidents, judges, and heads of government agencies. Some regulators also classify close family members and associates of PEPs as PEPs due to their potential influence.

PEPs are considered high-risk customers, not because of sanctions compliance, but due to their position and the potential for corruption. However, some high-ranking officials, such as heads of state, may also appear on OFAC's sanctions lists.

OFAC does not require companies to screen for PEPs, but identifying them is integral to an effective customer due diligence program. In the US and many other countries, AML (anti-money laundering) regulations mandate the identification and enhanced monitoring of PEPs. If your company is subject to AML regulations, you should already be conducting these checks.

A key challenge with PEP screening is determining how long someone remains a PEP after leaving office. There is no universal standard, but a common guideline is two years.

We screened for PEPs using our sanctions screening system. While OFAC does not provide a PEP list, most screening vendors include one. Doing business with a PEP is not prohibited, but you should carefully assess any corruption or AML red flags, especially regarding their transactions or source of funds.

Most regulations focus on foreign PEPs, not domestic ones. We initially monitored both but found that tracking US PEPs generated a high volume of alerts with little value—after all, PEPs need insurance, too.

Third-Party Due Diligence

Similar due diligence steps should be performed on vendors and third parties such as wholesalers, suppliers, and distributors. As part of your vendor contracting process, request the following information to vet for any sanctions issues:

- name and location of the company
- ownership of the company
- ultimate beneficial owners of the company (if different from ownership)
- if any executives or board members are on any sanctions watchlists
- what countries they will be working on your company's contract in
- any sanctions-related investigations, fines, or judgments in the last five years

In addition to reviewing the vendor's answers to these questions, you should conduct an independent negative news search for any sanctions-related issues in the last five years.

Realize that some companies will use subsidiaries or branches in other countries to perform the contract work. You need to identify those countries to verify that they do not have trade embargoes or other sanctions issues.

However, vendor management doesn't end after the contracting phase. If the contract with the vendor lasts for several years, you should perform ongoing monitoring. The frequency will depend on the vendor's risk. Less frequent monitoring can be done on smaller contracts with US companies. More frequent reviews (such as annually) should be conducted for large contracts where companies perform key activities (such as payment processing) overseas. During your periodic monitoring, verify that the information you gathered at onboarding is up-to-date, rescan all the names against the watchlists, conduct a negative news review for the time since onboarding, and verify the countries where the work is being performed have not become sanctioned.

Depending on the services your third-party vendor provides, you may need to regularly monitor them to ensure they are properly screening for sanctions compliance. For example, if you outsource payment processing, you should periodically review their screening process to ensure it meets your requirements.

12
Sanctions Clauses

One of the most important tools for staying compliant with sanctions is including exclusion clauses in contracts and insurance policies. These clauses state that the contract or policy is void if a sanctions violation occurs, helping you avoid paying for or covering prohibited transactions. Another clause could forbid the resale of your goods to countries where selling them is banned.

OFAC said, "The best and most reliable approach for insuring global risks without violating US sanctions law is to insert in global insurance policies an explicit exclusion for risks that would violate US sanctions law... It essentially shifts the risk of loss for the underlying transaction back to the insured - the person more likely to have direct control over the economic activity giving rise to the contact with a sanctioned country, entity or individual."[54]

In reality, you must not engage in any transaction that violates economic sanctions, even if that's not explicitly stated in your contract. However, including such a clause can offer you legal protection in a dispute, provide a basis for OFAC to reduce fines, and notify the contracted party that they won't be covered in situations where sanctions are violated.

You will want to enlist an attorney to ensure your sanctions clauses are valid and well-worded to protect you.

Sanctions exclusion language should be consistent across all documents and contracts to prevent gaps or discrepancies. You may want to include the approved exclusion language in your economic sanctions policy to ensure consistency.

Contracts

Several different types of contracts would benefit from a sanctions exclusion clause.

When contracting with a vendor for services, ensure the contract mandates compliance with sanctions and that they cannot become sanctioned or payment will not be made under the contract. Consider adding language requiring them to report any sanctions violations to you as part of your ongoing vendor monitoring process.

Similarly, if goods are sold to a third party, like a wholesaler, the contract should specify that the goods cannot be resold in a way that breaches sanctions, such as selling to a sanctioned party or country.

If your contract or the contract participants cover multiple jurisdictions, the sanctions exclusion clause should list the regions where a sanctions violation would void the contract. Clarifying which legal jurisdiction governs your contract is crucial because sanctions regulations vary between jurisdictions, affecting what's permissible. For instance, if you're under US jurisdiction and the transaction could breach US but not UK sanctions, you wouldn't want a clause that only covers compliance with UK sanctions regulations.

Typically, your sanctions exclusion clause would state that the contract becomes invalid if it breaches laws in any of these jurisdictions: your own, the contractor's, and the jurisdiction(s) where the transactions are conducted. Specifying these countries ensures there's no debate about invoking the sanctions clause if an OFAC violation occurs.

Insurance Policies

For insurance companies, your policies should have language that excludes coverage for sanctioned parties or losses and prohibits claims payments if they violate sanctions.

There may be a sanctions exclusion clause in your own personal insurance policies.

We based our sanctions exclusion language on Lloyd's LMA3100 form.[55] Lloyd's is a London insurance market, and their sanctions exclusion language is widely accepted. The language states that the insurer isn't liable for any claim and is not required to provide any coverage under the policy to the extent that it would expose the insurer to sanctions.

This language should be included in all policies, either directly in the contract, as an endorsement, or as a separate notice. How you incorporate the language depends on how easily your forms can be updated and whether those forms must be resubmitted for state review. You may want to use a notice, for example, if revisions to the form would cause a state to reopen and review the entire policy contract language, which could lead to a lot of avoidable work!

Sanctions Clauses Are Not Foolproof

Be aware, however, that sanctions clauses may not fully protect you in legal disputes.

The EU and the UK have "blocking statutes"[56] barring compliance with OFAC sanctions that conflict with their own (such as those for Iran and Cuba). This aims to protect UK and EU companies from extraterritorial laws and allow them to conduct business freely.

While the UK and EU governments won't sue US companies for using sanctions clauses, affected companies can bring civil cases against them.

Recent court cases have shown mixed outcomes.

In 2018, the UK High Court ruled insurers aren't liable to pay a claim when payments violate sanctions laws.[57] The Court said the blocking statute did not apply as the sanctions exclusion clause was part of the contract, so the defendant relied on complying with a contractual provision rather than US sanctions laws.[58]

However, the court also said that payment requirements are only suspended, not eliminated. If sanctions change in the future where this is no longer a prohibited transaction, the transaction should be completed at that time. This could cause open claims or payments to linger indefinitely.

In 2019, the UK High Court sided with a defendant who refused payment due to OFAC sanctions. The court stated that the policy was clear about sanctions compliance, and the insured should have been aware of the risks.[59]

In 2020, a UK bank stopped making interest payments to a lender in Cyprus because the lender's owner had become an OFAC SDN. As a result, the lender was considered sanctioned under the 50 Percent Rule, and the bank was worried about facing US secondary sanctions. The defendant used a nonpayment clause in the facility agreement to justify this action. The English Court of Appeal decided that the bank could rely on this nonpayment clause because US secondary sanctions were considered a "mandatory provision of law," as stated in the clause. In this case, the risk of breaching US secondary sanctions was enough to enforce the clause.[60]

In 2021, however, the EU Court of Justice ruled that companies under EU jurisdiction can't take action solely to comply with US sanctions if it violates the EU's blocking statute. The company must prove it wasn't seeking to comply with US sanctions laws when it canceled the business but took action for another appropriate reason.[61]

While this section focused on EU and UK blocking statutes, be aware that other countries such as China, Canada, France, and Germany also have blocking statutes. Their enforcement of these statutes may differ from that of the UK and the EU.

How to Protect Your Organization

To protect your company from blocking statutes, consider the following:

- Excluding certain jurisdictions in your contracts. Add territorial exclusion clauses in your contracts to avoid transactions in places like Iran or Cuba alongside sanctions exclusion clauses. This is particularly important if you are a foreign company and the transaction could have a US nexus.
- Relying on other contract clauses. Use general non-compliance with laws and regulations clauses or other legal grounds for ending a contract instead of citing sanctions.
- Carefully documenting your business decisions when canceling business due to sanctions. The documentation must show solid reasons for terminating a business, and these reasons must not show an intention to comply with US laws.
- Applying for a specific OFAC license. You might consider applying for an OFAC license to conduct the transaction. However, you must first get permission (i.e., a license) from the UK or the EU authority to apply for an OFAC license, and these applications are public. If your customer sees you're trying to comply with US sanctions that conflict with UK or EU sanctions, it might sue you.

So, sanctions clauses can help your company avoid violations of OFAC sanctions and the associated fines, but they may not fully protect against lawsuits under other countries' blocking statutes.

13

Environmental Scanning

Think of environmental scanning (aka "e-scan") as how you, as the sanctions compliance professional, stay updated on changes in economic sanctions regulations.

Sanctions can change regularly, so you must monitor them daily for changes to the watchlists, updates to sanctions programs, or the implementation of new programs.

You should develop a written procedure documenting how you will conduct the scanning, record your findings, and develop and implement new processes responding to new regulations.

Documenting Your E-Scan

You should record the results of your e-scan. You can do this easily in a spreadsheet, or larger companies might have a risk management application you can use. Create a spreadsheet with columns for the date, the source, the title, a brief summary of the item, whether it's relevant to your company, whether the change is already in effect (some rules may start later), if procedures need updating, the plan to update them, and the date it's completed.

An example spreadsheet setup:

Item #	2024-01
Date	4/29/2024
Source	OFAC
Title	Issuance of Russia-related General License
Summary	GL 8I extended, allowing certain energy-related services to be provided to specific Russian companies.
Effective?	Yes
Applicable?	Yes
Procedure Updates Needed?	No
Plan	Contact appropriate staff to let them know this license has been extended, and we can continue to use it.
Date Completed	5/1/2024

How to Conduct Environmental Scanning

Set up automatic emails so you don't resort to manual searches on Google. Some good places to get updates:
- Sign up at OFAC's website to get emails when they update lists and programs: https://service.govdelivery.com/accounts/USTREAS/subscriber/new.
- The UK's Office of Financial Sanctions Implementation (OFSI), which administers UK sanctions, also has an automated email system. You can sign up here: https://ofsi.blog.gov.uk/subscribe/.
- Join an organization. The Association of Certified Anti-Money Laundering Specialists (ACAMS) has a large sanctions team. Membership fees are nominal but provide a wealth of sanctions-related information, webinars, and conferences. https://www.acams.org/en.
- Set up Google alerts for keywords such as "sanctions," "OFAC," "economic sanctions," "trade sanctions," and "sanctions fines."
- Consider subscription services. Moneylaundering.com (a separate subscription service of ACAMS) collects news articles on sanctions, anti-money laundering (AML), and bribery and corruption from various sources. They send daily email summaries of new articles. While it can be costly, it's valuable for larger companies. Alternatively, you can subscribe to other services like Bloomberg or Lexis Nexis, which also provide sanctions-related articles and allow you to set up alerts.

Compliance Bulletins

Once you identify a relevant e-scan item, you should email the affected people in your company to inform them of how it affects them and their sanctions procedures. We referred to this email as a Compliance Bulletin and sent it to the applicable compliance professionals and line of business management. The Bulletin detailed the information in the spreadsheet above and may have listed required follow-up action by the parties who received the email (such as updating their processes). If you request that people take specific actions, work with them on those updates and follow up later to ensure they were implemented.

Unless you have a small company with few people you need to update, it is best to use an automated risk management solution that will generate the bulletin to the appropriate staff.

14

Training

A sanctions program will not be effective without staff training.

Per OFAC, training should (i) provide job-specific knowledge, (ii) communicate to each employee their sanctions compliance responsibilities, and (iii) hold employees accountable through testing.[62]

Who Needs Training?

Everyone in a company likely needs basic sanctions knowledge and training. Some employees who encounter sanctions issues regularly may require more detailed training. Your sanctions policy should describe who will receive sanctions training, how often it will be rolled out, how it will be tracked, and who will provide it. Consider US sanctions-specific training for foreign staff in those jobs that encounter US business most frequently.

Of course, the SCO and sanctions compliance staff will need training. However, their training usually comes from external sources like professional webinars and conferences. These sessions provide up-to-date, in-depth knowledge crucial for their roles.

Other jobs that may require at least a basic working knowledge of sanctions include those that (this is not an exhaustive list):

- process a payment (such as a claim, an account withdrawal, or vendor payment)
- originate a payment on an account
- open new accounts
- underwrite policies or loans
- process funds received from an external party or customer
- conduct customer due diligence
- import or export goods
- conduct marine shipments
- contract with vendors or other business partners
- hire staff
- make sales of goods or services

Depending on your organization's size, you might collaborate with other business professionals in the line of business or compliance to decide which job roles need training. In larger companies, job titles can be generic, and these teams know more about what each role involves and if they would benefit from sanctions training.

You might also want to offer training to third-party providers who handle tasks like customer account setup or payment services (i.e., job tasks with a higher risk for possible sanctions violations). Alternatively, review the training they offer their staff to ensure it meets your sanctions compliance needs. If you can't do this review, share your company's Vendor Code of Conduct outlining your expectations for sanctions compliance.

What Type of Training Should I Provide?

When you mention "training," many imagine being stuck in a stuffy room for hours. But that's not how it's done anymore. People are busy, and in larger companies, they often face frequent training requirements. Aim to make sanctions training quick and painless. Training can come in various forms, all contributing to a strong sanctions training program.

A Formal Training Course

This will be the primary training for most company staff who need basic knowledge of sanctions. It can be conducted in person or online, using a PowerPoint course developed internally or an off-the-shelf program from a learning platform like True Office (now Learning Pool https://learningpool.com/). Regardless of the format, the training should be brief, ideally lasting no more than twenty to thirty minutes. The exception is for staff regularly dealing with sanctions issues (see Internal Training Webinars). Online self-study courses should include a test or knowledge check questions that staff must pass to successfully complete the course.

After setting baseline expectations for staff regarding sanctions via this formal course, the following activities can be used for additional training refreshers throughout the year.

Team Meetings

Manager emails may suffice for minor procedural changes or regulatory updates. My prior organization sent periodic manager emails with updates on various topics, and we occasionally included sanctions updates. Managers can then discuss the information in their next team meeting, ensuring it reaches all staff effectively.

Internal Training Webinars

You can hold periodic online live training sessions, like a Lunch and Learn. I've led sanctions-related sessions during these events. You can meet with specific groups to discuss sanctions issues that are relevant to them. These meetings might last up to an hour and provide detailed information tailored to higher-risk teams, such as those handling payments, account openings, policy underwriting, or claims processing.

E-Newsletters

Consider sending a regular sanctions e-newsletter to key staff members in your organization. It doesn't have to be frequent; every quarter or semi-annually may be sufficient. We did this at one time, but admittedly, it was tough to keep the list current because of staff changes. However, it may work better for smaller organizations.

Online Articles/Blog

If your organization uses an internal Microsoft SharePoint site or something similar, it's a great place to share info. You can post a refresher article on sanctions (don't forget to link to your sanctions policy!) or share updates on procedures or upcoming training sessions. Sanctions compliance might even have a SharePoint-type site where staff can subscribe for updates. We used SharePoint for a sanctions "resource site," where we posted several sanctions-related documents that staff could reference if they had questions. Our policy was posted there, as were slides from prior training, written procedures, summaries of sanctions programs for the US, the UK, and the EU, a listing of embargoed countries, and sanctions FAQs, among other documents.

How Often Should I Provide Training?

People in key roles with a sanctions nexus need at least annual training and likely a refresher or more intensive training during the year. For those who just need to know the basics, a refresher every two to three years should do. Your risk assessment can help decide who needs training and how often.

How Should I Roll It Out?

You can issue your training using several methods. The method you use depends on several factors, such as the size of your company, how many employees need training, and what technology is available to you.

- Automated rollout through a company's learning management system (LMS) is easiest. Large companies often have an LMS for various training needs. You can integrate your sanctions training into this system, whether it's developed in-house or off-the-shelf. This system automatically assigns the course to employees you select and sets a deadline, such as 30 days, to complete the training. It sends reminders if someone hasn't completed it on time. Plus, the course can include a test at the end for employees to pass, and the system tracks successful completion.
- A live online webinar is suitable for providing more detailed training on complex sanctions topics targeted at specific groups of employees. One positive is that this format allows the participants to ask clarifying questions of the presenter. You can also record these sessions for staff who couldn't make the live event or new employees.
- A PowerPoint (or similar) presentation distributed manually can be challenging to manage but is suitable for smaller organizations. You send the training materials via email to the relevant staff (or send a link to a shared internal site where the training is located), set a completion deadline, and then they or their manager inform you when it's been completed.

How Should I Document Completed Training?

If you have an LMS, the system automatically records who took the training. Periodically, you should run a report of everyone to whom the training has been rolled out and see who has completed it and who is overdue (where you may want to follow up personally). The spreadsheet is your documentation of who received the training, should someone request it.

For online webinars, you usually send out an invite to affected parties. Then, you can see who attends the meeting and check them off the list. You can follow up with those who didn't participate in the webinar by sending a copy of the recording.

For manual rollout, use a spreadsheet of all people assigned to the training and when they completed it. You may also want to retain the emails you received when someone reported they completed the training in case of questions.

15
Auditing/Testing

Auditing and testing are covered together in this chapter because they are both ways to ensure your program operates as expected. But they're actually two different processes, and you should use both to validate the effectiveness of your sanctions program.

Auditing

Audits check if current processes work effectively and are consistent with the expected procedures and regulatory requirements. They help find weaknesses in the program and recommend ways to fix them.[63]

Auditing should be performed by someone outside of the sanctions compliance function. In most cases, the internal audit group will conduct the audit, but it can also be done by external auditors or an internal compliance person who is not responsible for the program. Being independent allows for objectivity and a fresh perspective on the process.

Audits can be intensive and last for weeks. However, the good news is that sanctions compliance isn't usually audited annually. How often it happens depends on when the last audit was done, the results of that review, changes in risk, and the auditor's own assessment of the organization's risks (i.e., how sanctions risk compare to other risks within the company).

During the planning phase of the audit, the SCO and sanctions compliance team members will meet with auditors to discuss their processes and controls. They might walk the auditors through significant processes, like clearing alerts, and provide important documents, such as the policy and risk assessment. The auditors may create their own risk matrix or flowchart of the procedures and key controls.

At the end of the planning phase, the auditors will provide an engagement memo outlining the audit's scope and objectives. The scope is just what areas of the organization the audit will cover. In this case, it may be the sanctions compliance function and related processes, such as a review of IT controls over the automated scanning system. The objectives are the auditors' goals for the audit. For example, one objective may be to evaluate whether the sanctions compliance program is sufficient to prevent the organization from conducting prohibited transactions.

Once the engagement memo is issued, audit testing will commence. Audit testing will likely include the following elements:
- reviewing the SCP documents, such as the policy, risk assessment, and key written procedures
- sample testing of certain transactions to ensure a sanctions scan was conducted
- sample testing of alerts to validate they are cleared appropriately
- evaluating positive matches identified to verify they were handled according to written procedures
- reviewing a sample of oversight activities (such as compliance testing as discussed in the following section) to ensure they are being conducted

Expect to meet with the auditors occasionally throughout the audit work to talk over any questions and findings they've identified to date. At the end of the audit, there will be a closing meeting, where auditors will discuss the findings in the report and suggest ways to fix any issues. "Findings" are simply potential weaknesses or gaps they've identified in the sanctions process, such as controls not performed consistently or being absent altogether.

Post-audit, the final report will be issued. Frequently, a rating of the sanctions compliance program will be included in the report. Potential ratings, which will vary by organization, include "effective," "partially effective," "significant improvement needed," and "ineffective." Obviously, you would rather have an effective program than an ineffective one. The audience for the report will usually include senior management. Sanctions compliance will be expected to remediate the gaps identified in the report, and the SCO should periodically report to senior management on the progress in resolving the findings.

Compliance Testing

Compliance testing differs from auditing in that it is ongoing and usually performed by the person responsible for overseeing the sanctions program.

This person could be the SCO or, more commonly, the manager of the sanctions compliance team.

Compliance testing involves sample-testing the performance of the internal controls to ensure they are functioning effectively. Your controls, and thus the tests you conduct, will vary, but below is a sample of some tests to consider:
- review payment reports to ensure funds aren't being sent to sanctioned countries
- reexamine a sample of cleared alerts to verify they are being reviewed within expected timeframes, clearing reasons are accurate, items are escalated when needed, and relevant documentation is attached
- scan reports of new foreign accounts opened or policies issued to verify no accounts exist in sanctioned countries
- analyze new vendor agreements, policies, or contracts to verify that sanctions exclusion language is included

You don't have to conduct every test each month. Set up a schedule based on risk. Maybe you review a sample of alerts cleared monthly and perform one or two other tests each quarter, for example.

You should document your review, perhaps with notes, initials, and date reviewed in reports or electronic documents.

CONDUCTING A RISK ASSESSMENT

16

Introduction to Risk Assessments

OFAC recommends that organizations take a risk-based approach to their sanctions compliance program (SCP). But what does that mean? To develop an effective SCP, you must evaluate and understand your company's specific sanctions challenges and vulnerabilities. This requires conducting a thorough assessment of your risk factors.

What Is Risk?

Per OFAC, sanctions risks are potential threats or vulnerabilities that, if ignored or not properly handled, can lead to violations of OFAC's regulations and negatively affect an organization's reputation and business.[64]

In other words, considering your company's unique situation, how likely are you to violate sanctions regulations when conducting business?

What Is a Risk Assessment and Why Is it Important?

A sanctions risk assessment (SRA) is a method for identifying, analyzing, and addressing a company's exposure to sanctions-related risks. It helps pinpoint weaknesses in compliance programs and lays out a plan to fix them. The primary goal of an SRA is to evaluate and reduce the risk of sanctions violations, ensuring compliance with OFAC regulations. By identifying gaps and strengthening controls, an SRA ensures compliance with OFAC regulations, minimizes financial penalties for violations, and protects an entity's reputation in the marketplace.

Who Should Conduct One?

All entities should conduct an SRA, particularly those at higher risk for sanctions violations, such as:

- companies that conduct business internationally, including professional services such as law, accounting, and consulting
- financial institutions such as banks, cryptocurrency firms, broker-dealers, mutual funds, and insurance companies
- businesses that sell, import, export, or ship goods

- entities that work as governmental contractors

However, all businesses, including small, single-owner entities, can benefit from even a basic assessment of their sanctions risk exposure.

Depending on its size, an entity can have multiple levels of SRAs. First and foremost, all organizations should have an enterprise-wide SRA encompassing all risks and controls for the entire company. However, individual departments or divisions within larger companies may assess their sanctions risk separately ("sub-assessments") as part of an overall departmental risk assessment. The sanctions risks and controls identified in those sub-assessments should roll up into the enterprise-wide risk assessment.

Introduction to the Risk Assessment Case Study

As we progress through this guide, we will create a basic enterprise risk assessment for a fictional company. This company has implemented some sanctions controls, but no formal risk and controls assessment has been conducted.

Here is the link to download the final, completed risk assessment for our case study and a blank risk assessment template to use as you embark on your own SRA: https://easysanctions.wordpress.com/the-plain-english-guide-to-economic-sanctions-risk-assessments/.

17
Steps in the Risk Assessment Process

OFAC recommends that an entity develop a methodology to identify, analyze, and address its sanctions risks.[65] There is no one approach to conducting a risk assessment. However, the following steps, explained in detail in the following chapters, provide a framework to identify and analyze all possible risks. This method will also allow an organization to take a holistic (i.e., entire entity) view of the company from top to bottom.

1. Scoping the business–Chapter 18
2. Identifying risk categories–Chapter 19
3. Identifying sanctions risks–Chapter 20
4. Establishing the risk criteria–Chapter 21
5. Calibrating the risk score–Chapter 22
6. Assessing risks–Chapter 23
7. Identifying controls–Chapter 24
8. Assessing controls–Chapter 25
9. Gap identification and remediation–Chapter 26
10. Documenting the risk assessment/next steps–Chapter 27

The Plain-English Guide to Economic Sanctions Risk Assessments Workbook can also assist you in completing your first risk assessment with easy-to-use worksheets that cover every step in the process.

18
Scoping

The most important part of your risk assessment is the information-gathering phase, also known as "scoping." You can't conduct a risk assessment without first understanding all parts of your company. This means you must begin by identifying all your organization's legal entities, business teams, functional units, departments and divisions, customers, products, services, supply chains, geographies, etc.

There are three ways to collect this information on your entity:

- document gathering
- questionnaires
- meetings or interviews

Document Gathering

The best way to start your SRA project is to obtain as much information about your company as possible. This may include internal organizational charts, a listing of all legal entities, regulatory filings (such as with the SEC if you work for a public company), annual and semi-annual reports, procedure documents, information on what products you provide, your distribution channels, and where you do business.

These items may be readily available on your company's external website or an internal site (such as SharePoint). Otherwise, you may need to request them from co-workers. These documents will help you identify who to contact to get your questions answered and provide more specificity to your questions.

Questionnaires

A questionnaire should be developed to gather the information from each business unit you contact. While not all questions will be relevant for every department, a questionnaire will help ensure consistency of information collected and that no topics are overlooked with any group.

A sample questionnaire is included with the risk assessment template and gathers details on the risk criteria discussed in Chapter 21. You may need to define some terms in the questionnaire. For example, "dual-use goods," a well-known term in sanctions, won't be familiar to most people.

You'll also want information about the type of data the business unit handles (like customer information, financial transactions, and sales data) and which system the data is stored on. This will assist you in verifying that you are scanning all pertinent data against OFAC watchlists.

In larger organizations, you may want to begin your SRA process by sending out the questionnaire for completion. After it is returned, you can contact the person who completed the questionnaire with any follow-up questions by email, phone, or meeting.

Meetings/Interviews

In smaller organizations, you may be able to meet (either face-to-face or virtually) with a representative from each unit of the company and address the questions in person. Meetings will also be most effective for questionnaire responses that require deeper dives.

Who Should Be Contacted

Every department within your company, including foreign locations, should be included in your risk assessment. If you don't know somebody in a unit, start with the manager and request someone to be your liaison for the SRA project. Don't forget to include corporate units such as accounts payable, information technology, and human resources in your risk assessment. Sanctions risk exists there, too.

Senior Management Buy-in

An SRA is a labor-intensive endeavor and involves multiple people across the company. Implementing changes resulting from the SRA will also necessitate employee buy-in on the new processes. That's why it's essential to have senior management support for your risk assessment project. With senior management "sponsorship," employees contacted for your SRA project will understand they are expected to assist you.

At the outset of your SRA, have a senior manager (such as the chief compliance officer) email managers who report to them announcing the start of the sanctions risk assessment and that their teams' cooperation with the project is expected. This will smooth the way for contacting other employees for information. This will also demonstrate senior management's commitment to sanctions compliance, as recommended by OFAC.[66]

Case Study: Background on WeExport

You work for WeExport, a fictional organization. From your initial scoping, you learned the following information:

WeExport has 2,500 employees in the US, the UK, and China. WeExport builds and sells computer parts for high-end computer systems used by governmental agencies, schools, and entities in the military, defense, and aerospace industries. Its revenue was $25 million last year. The entity in the UK is a sales office for foreign customers and is legally organized as a branch of WeExport. The China site is a manufacturing facility organized as a WeExport subsidiary.

You've identified the following departments within the company: sales, finance, human resources, legal and compliance, information technology (IT), shipping and receiving, customer service, marketing, product development, procurement, manufacturing, and the individual sales channels—government, education, and industry. WeExport also has a team of three people who conduct sanctions compliance activities and report to the chief compliance officer.

19
Risk Categories

Your questionnaire will consist of questions regarding specific risk categories.

What Is a Risk Category

In a risk assessment, a "risk category" is a classification used to group similar types of risks. These categories help to organize and prioritize potential threats or vulnerabilities based on their nature and impact on the organization. Grouping risks into categories makes it easier to systematically evaluate and manage them.

What Categories Should Be Assessed

As recommended by OFAC, you should gather detailed information on your **customers, products, services,** and **locations**. However, there are several other risk categories you should also include, depending on your type of business:

- supply chains
- distribution channels
- counterparties/third-party associates
- types of transactions
- governmental contracts
- technology

For larger entities, you may want to assess these items at the corporate level and separately by business unit or location. For example, at my previous company, we separately evaluated the risk categories for our foreign entities and distinct business units of our domestic entities, such as group benefits insurance, personal insurance, commercial insurance, and treasury. I then rolled those up into an assessment at the corporate level.

At the most basic level, the goal is to identify which of your risk categories—or which items within those categories—pose the highest threat of a sanctions violation.

As discussed in the prior chapter, you gather information on these risk categories via your questionnaire, document review, and meetings.

When addressing these risk categories, you should also try to quantify them. For example, suppose you learn that customers primarily come from the government, education, and defense industries. In that case, you will want to know the approximate percentage from each sector. This is because each industry has a different amount of associated sanctions risk. If most customers are in the defense industry, then the overall customer risk to the company would be considered higher than if most of the customers were educational.

Below are several questions to ask during the scoping phase. These questions are also included in the risk assessment template included with this guide.

Customers

- Who are your customers?
- Are they individuals, small businesses, governments, or corporations?
- Do you have a steady base of customers, or do most customers conduct one-off transactions?
- What industries or sectors do your customers operate in?

Businesses pose a higher risk than individuals because it's easier to conceal the true ownership of a company. A stable customer base poses less risk since you know their usual transaction patterns and can identify a transaction that is out of the ordinary. On the other hand, new clients are riskier because you're unfamiliar with them and the types of transactions they'll carry out.

The industry a customer operates in also affects their risk level. Customers in the military, defense, and technology sectors pose a higher sanctions risk than those in the food and clothing sectors. This is because OFAC imposes sanctions more often on military/defense industries and technological goods than on humanitarian items like food and clothing.

Keep in mind a customer can also be an internal department. Teams such as HR and IT will have internal, not external, customers. These customers should also be captured in your questionnaire.

Products

- Do you provide goods or services, or both?
- What specific products and services do you sell?
- Are the products considered "dual-use goods" (used for civilian and military purposes)?

Identify the various types of products you sell, as they carry different risk levels. For instance, if you sell financial products, allowing online account opening poses a higher risk than those requiring in-person verification. Similarly, certain goods may entail greater risk depending on their industry use. For example, office chairs typically pose a low risk. In contrast, laptops may pose a higher risk if your customers are military contractors rather than schools.

If you provide a service as your "product," consider whether the service is high-risk or is used by high-risk customers. For example, a business offering payday loans has a higher sanctions risk than plumbing services. For an internal department, such as finance, their "product" may be providing wire and ACH services or receiving payment for goods, transactions which can affect your company's sanctions risk.

Services

- What services do you offer your customers?
- How are your services delivered?

Services here differ from whether your product is a service.

Do you provide correspondent banking services, online account setup, Automated Clearing House (ACH), or wire transactions? All of these may pose a higher risk. Additionally, extending credit to your customers can also increase risk.

How services are provided also impacts risk. Online transactions or services handled by third-party providers are riskier than in-person services provided by company employees. When you offer services online, it's harder to be sure who you're actually doing business with.

Geographic Jurisdiction

- Where do you have employees?

- Where do you do business (sell goods, have offices, or provide services)?
- Do you have any business partners (vendors, etc.) in foreign locations?
- What countries specifically?

Each country carries its own sanctions risk. Business conducted in higher-risk jurisdictions (explained more fully in Chapter 23) poses an elevated risk of sanctions violations to your company. You will want to identify what countries your products or services are sold in and a breakdown of its largest jurisdictions. For example, if you decide that China is a high-risk jurisdiction for your company, but only .01 percent of your sales are made there, will you want to focus all of your sanctions controls on that business? Or will you want to focus more on Russia, which is also considered a higher-risk jurisdiction, where 20 percent of your sales are?

Remember that there can be differences in risk even within the United States. Areas of the US can be considered higher risk due to drug trafficking or money laundering concerns.

Supply Chains

- What suppliers do you use, and what components or materials do they supply?
- Do the suppliers source materials from foreign countries?
- Do the suppliers source materials from other entities?
- Where are your primary suppliers located (in what countries specifically)?
- Who engages or contracts with these suppliers?
- Who oversees these suppliers?

Suppliers can pose a high sanctions risk for an entity because they may get their source materials from sanctioned countries or providers, and you may not be aware of it. Foreign suppliers, specifically, may not need to comply with OFAC and may not be familiar with all the prohibitions. OFAC has fined companies that use those prohibited materials in their goods.[67] And yes, OFAC expects you to vet every company in the supply chain. So, if your supplier gets materials from a company that sources part of it from elsewhere, you must document all that information in the SRA questionnaire to assess that risk.

It is also possible that whoever engaged the supplier did not thoroughly review the supplier at the outset of the contract, including where they obtain their materials. A business unit engaging suppliers directly poses a greater concern than a separate procurement group whose job is to vet potential third-party partners for risk.

Someone within the company, whether in the business line or a procurement team, should oversee the contract and ensure compliance with its terms, including any clauses related to compliance with OFAC sanctions.

Distribution Channels / Wholesalers

- What channels do you distribute goods through?
- Do you use any distributors in foreign countries, and if so, what countries specifically?
- Do distribution channels go through any countries with trade embargoes (Iran, Syria, North Korea, Cuba, Russia, or Russian-held areas of Ukraine)?
- Who engages or contracts with these distributors, and what criteria are used to select them?
- Who oversees these distributors?

Distributors and wholesalers, similar to suppliers, can pose a high sanctions risk for an entity because they may sell your products in embargoed countries, to sanctioned entities, or in countries where that specific good is prohibited for export. In addition, the distributor or wholesaler is an intermediary between you and your customer. This may prevent an organization from knowing its customers well enough to identify if they are a sanctions concern, causing the company to rely on the distributor or wholesaler to conduct sufficient due diligence. Also, foreign distributors and wholesalers may not need to comply with OFAC and may not be familiar with all the prohibitions.

OFAC will penalize companies if their goods are sold in a prohibited manner. For example, your wholesaler in the Middle East could sell your products in Iran, where a US company is prohibited from exporting them, resulting in OFAC fines.[68]

Like a supplier, it is possible that whoever engaged the third party did not thoroughly review them at the outset of the contract, including where and to whom they sell or ship your goods. A business unit engaging third parties directly poses a greater concern than a separate procurement team whose job is to vet potential third-party partners for risk.

Someone within the company, whether in the business line or a procurement team, should oversee the contract and ensure compliance with its terms, including any clauses related to compliance with OFAC sanctions and where your company's goods can and can't be sold.

Counterparties/Third-Party Associates

- Do you use any third-party business partners, including counterparties and vendors?
- What services do these third parties provide?
- Are any located in foreign countries, or do they provide services in foreign countries (what countries specifically)?
- Who engages or contracts with these third parties, and what criteria are used to select them?
- Who oversees these third parties?
- Do any of these third parties use subcontractors?

Counterparties, vendors, and third-party business partners (such as law firms or consultants) pose similar risks to suppliers and distribution partners. Suppose a vendor subcontracts some of the services they provide to you, and the subcontractor operates in a foreign country. This can pose a higher sanctions risk to your company than if the contractor provided the services themselves. At my previous firm, one vendor subcontracted work to independent contractors in Belarus. After the start of the Russian conflict, when Belarus became subject to sanctions, we had to decide if we wanted that exposure.

Additionally, a third party operating on your company's behalf in a foreign country (like a consulting firm hired to generate business) increases your company's risk. They might do business with sanctioned parties or governments or bribe other entities to bring you business.

Types of Transactions

- What transactions are conducted by the department?
- What is the volume of the transactions?
- What is the value of the transactions (high, medium, low)?
- What is the frequency of customer transactions (regular/routine, sporadic, or one-off)?
- Can transactions be conducted on behalf of third parties or anonymous parties?
- Can the transaction have a counterparty, beneficiary, or intermediary (in other words, does the transaction involve or is for the benefit of someone other than your customer)?
- Are any transactions conducted in cash or cryptocurrency?
- Are any transactions (such as electronic funds transfers) to or from foreign countries?

Transactions involve the transfer of goods, services, or funds. They can pose an elevated sanctions risk to an organization if they involve a foreign country, a foreign bank, or a third party, such as an intermediary or counterparty you have not vetted.

Sanctioned parties will often use an intermediary to conduct transactions on their behalf. If a customer buys goods to be shipped to a country where they don't operate or buys goods that don't match their business (like a fashion retailer purchasing circuit boards), it could be a red flag that they're acting for an unknown third party.

High-value transactions can involve more risk, as they are usually for higher-value goods that sanctioned parties or money launderers may desire.

Cash and cryptocurrency transactions are high risk because you don't know where the funds came from or who they are going to. Cash and cryptocurrency are popular methods sanctioned parties and criminals use to conduct transactions.

Finally, consider the volume of these transactions. Do your customers engage in many transactions or just a few? That can also affect risk.

Government Contracts

- Does the firm contract with federal, state, or foreign governments to provide goods or services?
- What foreign governments do you have contracts with?

Government contracts may be considered low risk, but they can still be a sanctions threat to your company. For example, your agreement with the government may state that you can't do business with certain parties that may or may not be sanctioned. My last company was a government contractor. In some cases, we had to certify that we weren't doing business with specific entities with ties to China or the Iran energy sector, some of which were not sanctioned by OFAC.

In some instances, the entire country (such as Iran), a governmental regime (such as the government of Venezuela), or specific governmental departments (such as the Myanmar Directorate of Procurement in Myanmar/Burma) may be sanctioned, which can present difficulty in identifying allowable governmental business.

In addition, an organization has to exercise more caution in negotiating these contracts to ensure nothing is offered or received that could be considered a bribe under US or local regulations. Foreign governmental entities can include state-owned enterprises, such as hospitals or universities, that may be your target customers.

Technology

- What data does your department maintain (customer data, transactions, vendor information, account data, sales data, etc.)?
- What application or system is this data maintained on?

These questions will help you identify the data you need to scan and verify it is being checked against sanctions watchlists.

Case Study: Risk Categories for WeExport

Conducting the SRA for WeExport, you've obtained the following information:

Customers: IT companies that build high-end computers for governments, education, and defense/military/aerospace industries.

Approximately 45 percent of the business is defense/military/aerospace, 25 percent is other government, 15 percent is education, and 15 percent in miscellaneous industries. Customers are relatively stable as a limited number of well-known companies are building these systems. WeExport does not conduct a beneficial ownership review of any of its customers.

Products: Parts used in high-end computers. They can be considered dual-use goods.

Services: WeExport provides warranty and repair services through third-party vendors.

Geographic Jurisdiction: Products are sold to US-based (approximately 50 percent) and foreign customers. Of the foreign customers, China is the largest purchaser (25 percent). Other countries include Canada, India, Germany, and South Africa.

Suppliers: WeExport has three suppliers for materials for its computer parts, two of which are in China and India. The one in China has a third-party supplier that it can use to source materials.

Distributors/Wholesalers: WeExport uses three distributors/wholesalers in the US, Germany, and the Middle East.

Third Parties: WeExport outsources payroll and IT services. IT services are conducted from India.

Transactions: Frequent, regular, medium-sized bulk purchases of computer parts. Medium dollar value transactions as the parts are not high-value items. Transactions are not always with the final beneficial owner of the goods, as wholesalers are involved.

Governmental Contracts: WeExport has contracts with the US government and France.

Technology: An automated scanning system has been implemented. Employee data in the HR system and vendor onboarding data in their procurement system are not being scanned against sanctions watchlists. Payments to vendors and other third parties, such as wholesalers and distributors, are scanned via their accounts payable system, and customer names are checked when an order is placed.

20
Sanctions Risks

Now that you have identified and gathered information on your company's risk categories, you need to identify the specific sanctions-related risks your company may face.

Sanctions Risk

As mentioned earlier, sanctions risk refers to potential threats or weaknesses that can lead to violations of OFAC regulations if not properly managed by internal controls.

Sanctions risks are different from risk categories. Risk categories influence the sanctions risk score, either raising or lowering it.

Identifying Sanctions Risks

Brainstorm all the ways your organization could violate sanctions without any controls in place. This will be your universe of risks that you have to mitigate.

Some sanctions risks that your company may face include (this is not an exhaustive list):

- The company's sanctions compliance program is insufficient to comply with economic sanctions.
- The company does not identify sanctions issues.
- Sanctioned customers are not identified.
- Transactions that violate sanctions are conducted.
- Technology is insufficient to enable sanctions compliance.
- Employees don't understand sanctions.
- Required OFAC reports are not filed.
- The company does not block assets of an SDN or reject a transaction for an SDN when required by the regulation.
- New sanctions requirements are not identified and implemented.
- Third parties may put the company at risk for sanctions violations.
- Documents are not retained for the required amount of time.

Broken Controls

When framing sanctions risks in your SRA, ensure they are not phrased as broken controls (i.e., a missing or defective control). For example, "we don't scan our customers" is not a risk but a broken control. The risk is "sanctioned customers are not identified" or "we do business with sanctioned parties." Scanning would be a way to control those risks, and not performing it is a gap. Another example is "employees aren't trained in sanctions." That is, again, a broken control, the control being "training." The actual risk is that employees don't understand sanctions, so they don't follow procedures.

In the next chapter, we'll begin discussing how to assign values to the risk categories and the sanctions risks.

Case Study: Sanctions Risks for WeExport

WeExport identified the sanctions risks bulleted above as the sanctions risks for their company.

21
Risk Criteria

Now that we have identified our risk categories and sanctions risks, we must establish how to measure them. This is done using risk criteria. This chapter will discuss the criteria for assessing the risk categories, sanctions risks, and controls.

What Are Risk Criteria

Risk criteria are the measures used to evaluate the significance of a risk. In a risk assessment, this includes inherent risk, residual risk, likelihood, and severity.

Inherent Risk

Inherent risk is the risk level before implementing any controls. In simpler terms, it's how likely a sanctions violation will occur without controls. It takes into consideration both the likelihood and severity of a risk. For example, a company with high-risk customers, products, services, and geography might have a high inherent risk level for the sanctions risk: "sanctioned customers are not identified." A local retail business would likely have a low inherent risk for the same risk since they would have less exposure to higher-risk customers and locations.

Residual Risk

Residual risk is the likelihood that a sanctions violation will occur after the controls are performed. Your goal is that the controls will reduce the inherent risk. A company with a high inherent risk for "sanctioned customers are not identified" may find that their residual risk falls to medium or even low with robust, effective controls. A company with few or ineffective controls may find the residual risk remains high.

If the residual risk remains outside your risk tolerance with the current controls, then procedures must be redesigned to be more effective, or new processes must be developed. However, your goal is not to completely eliminate all risk, as that would not be possible.

Risk tolerance is how much risk you are willing to have in your sanctions program, considering the potential for violations. For example, a residual risk of high may not fall within your tolerance (and it shouldn't), but a medium residual risk may be acceptable.

Although not all assessments include them, the following two criteria can also be used in your risk assessment. They will assist you in evaluating your company's risks more accurately.

Likelihood

Likelihood is the probability of a risk occurring. It is related to inherent risk, but not the same. For the local retailer example above, you may have a high inherent risk for the sanctions risk: "sanctioned customers are not identified" as you don't have any sanctions controls in place. However, being a store that operates primarily locally, the likelihood of encountering a customer or transaction with a sanctions nexus is low. Assessing both criteria will help you design the appropriate level of control for your risks.

You may not want to focus on risks with a low likelihood of occurrence and focus your initial efforts on those with a high likelihood. You will use the assessment of your risk categories to determine the likelihood of a sanctions risk violation. For example, if you have assessed the customer risk as high, the likelihood of a violation for the risk "sanctioned customers are not identified" is likely or highly likely.

Severity

Severity is the potential impact or consequences of a sanctions-related violation. This includes financial losses, legal penalties, reputational damage, and operational disruptions. Assessing severity helps organizations understand the seriousness of each risk and prioritize their mitigation efforts accordingly.

For example, you may decide that the severity of the sanctions risk, "the company's sanctions compliance program is insufficient to comply with economic sanctions," is critical because a violation would likely lead to significant legal penalties, reputational damage from an OFAC fine, possible legal fees for lawsuits, and operational disruptions as you work quickly to fix the program.

To quantify severity, look at prior published OFAC notices and see what the fines were, what the aggravating factors were (aggravating factors increase the penalty, which is a concern if you have the same control gap), and what types of violations were publicized (not all OFAC violations lead to a public notice). You can do Google searches to see what publicity is generated when a company is fined to assess possible reputational impact. Also, consider if you have to report violations in public filings, such as annual reports or SEC filings. You can even use prior litigation or penalties your company received in the past as a benchmark.

Some companies prepare a formal matrix (sometimes called a "heat map") and mark where each of the sanctions risk categories falls. I have included a template for one in the risk assessment template, although there are several examples on the internet.[69]

22
Risk Scores

Before we begin assessing the risks, we have one last step—defining how we measure our risk categories (Chapter 19), sanctions risks (Chapter 20), and risk criteria (Chapter 21). This is done using a risk score.

What Is a Risk Score

A risk score is a categorical value assigned to a risk based on its assessed impact and likelihood. This score helps prioritize which risks need immediate attention and action.

When the risk categories, sanctions risks, and risk criteria are assessed, they are scored as high, medium, or low, which will determine the company's overall risk level. I also recommend using medium-high and medium-low for larger companies with diverse risks that need more precise measurement.

Below are general definitions of high, medium, and low risk:

High risk: Indicates the significant possibility of a sanctions violation occurring in the current state. Includes a substantial potential for severe consequences. These risks require urgent attention and robust controls to mitigate them.

Medium risk: Denotes a moderate possibility of a sanctions violation occurring in the current state with a modest potential for financial or reputational impact. These risks need regular monitoring and adequate controls but are less urgent than high risks.

Low risk: Suggests a low likelihood of occurrence in the current state with a minimal potential financial or reputational impact. These risks require routine checks but generally do not need immediate or intensive controls.[70]

To assess likelihood and severity, you can use the high/medium/low scale to stay consistent with how inherent and residual risks are evaluated and to avoid confusion. However, we will use the more commonly used scores in this guide. Likelihood is scored from highly likely to possible to highly unlikely, and severity ranges from negligible to medium to critical. These scores generally correspond to the aforementioned high, medium, and low definitions.

23
Assessing Risks

Using the risk categories from Chapter 19, the sanctions risks from Chapter 20, the risk criteria from Chapter 21, and the risk scores from Chapter 22, you are now ready to assess your organization's sanctions-related risks.

How Risk Score Is Determined

The sanctions risk for each criterion must be assessed and given a score of high, medium, and low to arrive at the company's final risk level. So, the question on your mind is likely: How do I determine whether something is high, medium, or low risk? This will differ from entity to entity and is a somewhat subjective determination based on the assessor's knowledge of sanctions and familiarity with the company and its industry. It can depend on factors such as the financial impact, whether there would be publicity, whether your company operates globally, and whether the industries it operates in are frequently targeted for sanctions.

For example, you may decide that a risk is low if it involves a loss of under five thousand dollars, does not require reporting, and is unlikely to be publicized. On the other hand, you may decide a risk is high if it would involve a penalty of over $1 million, lead to potential lawsuits, and be publicized globally.

Making this assessment more complicated, a spectrum of risks may be identifiable within the same category. For example, some customers (individuals) may be at lower risk than others (military customers). This is why it's essential to try and quantify these risk categories. If 95 percent of your customers are individuals, your customer risk will be lower than if 95 percent of your customers are military customers.

For those without experience with risk assessments, the **Federal Financial Institutions Examination Council (FFIEC)**[71] BSA/AML Manual has a suitable, easy-to-read matrix with examples of what to consider high, medium, or low. OFAC also uses this matrix.[72]

Assess the risk categories first, then use those assessments to analyze the sanctions risks. You should also consider assessing risk by individual departments or business units to identify those parts of the organization with higher sanctions risk.

Risk Category Analysis

Let's apply these criteria to a sample of our WeExport risk categories in Table 1. Your assessment of these risk categories may differ, and that's perfectly acceptable. Remember, a significant part of this process is subjective. The key takeaway from this exercise is to stimulate your thinking about all the different factors and how they interact to determine the risk rating for a company.

Table 1. Risk Category Analysis for WeExport

Risk Category	Risk Score & Rationale
Customers	medium-high
	Most of WeExport's customers are businesses that build high-end computers for governments, education, and defense/military/aerospace industries. Nearly half of the business is in a high-risk industry. Some products are sold through wholesalers, making the ultimate end user unknown to WeExport. This initially suggests high customer risk. However, the other customer categories are not considered at high risk for sanctions. Also, WeExport has determined that customers are relatively stable, with a limited, well-known number of companies building these types of systems. These factors lower the risk. However, since WeExport does not conduct beneficial ownership reviews of its customers or identify those sold to by wholesalers, customer risk is considered medium-high.
Product	high
	The product, computer parts, falls in a category frequently restricted by OFAC across various sanctions programs. These goods are often used in sanctioned industries like the military and defense, making them dual-use goods. Therefore, the product risk is considered high.

Table 1 (continued).

Risk Category	Risk Score & Rationale
Geography	medium-high
	WeExport operates globally, with manufacturing in China, a higher-risk country. They also have distributors, wholesalers, and suppliers in foreign countries, including higher-risk areas like China, India, and the Middle East. Half of their products are sold to US-based entities, reducing geographic risk. Among the other countries that procure their goods, China is the highest-risk location, with about 25 percent of sales. This means 75 percent of their products are sold in lower-risk regions, reducing the overall risk. However, their domestic and foreign wholesalers can sell to customers and countries unknown to WeExport, so the geographic risk remains medium-high.
Third Parties	medium-high
	Two of WeExport's suppliers are in China and India, considered higher-risk jurisdictions. Additionally, WeExport has one distributor/wholesaler in a high-risk area (the Middle East). The company also outsources payroll and IT services, with one subcontracted to a facility in India. WeExport considers the number of third parties it uses to be average for its industry. However, using third parties for distribution and supplies, including one in a high-risk area, increases the risk because there is less visibility into the other parties involved in the transaction. While China and India are higher-risk jurisdictions, they are not the highest-risk areas globally. This, along with the moderate number of outsourcing relationships, puts the risk in the medium-high range.
Transactions	medium-high
	WeExport has frequent, regular, medium-sized bulk purchases of goods. Most transactions are with parties whom WeExport deals with regularly, so they are transacting with mostly known parties. The dollar value per transaction is medium-sized. All this points to a medium risk. However, WeExport doesn't accept cash but will accept cryptocurrency in certain instances, which is the highest-risk payment method because criminals often use it due to its anonymity. This raises the risk to medium-high.

Reviewing the risk scores for these categories, it appears so far that WeExport probably has an overall sanctions risk in the medium-high range. Let's next look at the sanctions risks.

Sanctions Risks Analysis

Now, we will assess the inherent risk, likelihood, and severity of each sanctions risk for the WeExport case study. I have selected a few of the sanctions risks identified in Chapter 20 for analysis in Table 2. The remainder are included in the completed SRA.

Table 2. Sanctions risk analysis for WeExport

Sanctions Risk	Inherent Risk	Likelihood	Severity
Employees don't understand sanctions or follow sanctions procedures.	High	Highly likely	Critical
	Sanctions are complex regulations, and most employees don't work with them or receive training on them. Therefore, the likelihood of employees not understanding sanctions is high. WeExport's risk categories were assessed to be in the medium-high range, making employee knowledge of sanctions vital to compliance. This will lead to a high likelihood of a sanctions violation, incurring high fines and penalties.		
Third parties may put the company at risk for sanctions violations.	Medium-high	Likely	Medium
	WeExport works with several third parties for supplies, sales, and outsourced processes, some of which are in foreign countries not subject to OFAC regulations. The number of third parties is not high, and most are not in high-risk areas. Therefore, the probability of a violation occurring is likely rather than highly likely because the number of suppliers, distributors, and third-party vendors is moderate. An OFAC violation by a third party would expose WeExport to fines and penalties, reputational risk, and potential for lawsuits. Since most transactions are moderate in size and value, the severity of a penalty would likely be less monetarily than higher-value transactions.		

Table 2 (continued).

Sanctions Risk	Inherent Risk	Likelihood	Severity
Required documents are not retained for the required amount of time.	Medium-low	Unlikely	Low
	Companies, including WeExport, function in a digital environment and naturally have computer systems in place that save documents that have been created. Therefore, the probability of a pertinent sanctions-related document not being available when necessary is low. If sanctions-related documentation is unavailable during an OFAC inquiry or when assessing a possible violation, that would increase the risk of fines and penalties, increasing the severity. However, basic computerization would manage this risk, so severity is considered low.		
Sanctioned customers are not identified.	Medium-high	Highly likely	Critical
	WeExport has a mostly stable base of regular customers with whom they are familiar, so the risk isn't high. However, WeExport's customers are in high-risk industries and can be located in foreign countries. Also, they sell through third parties and rely on those entities to vet purchasers of WeExport's goods, which increases risk. The probability of a sanctioned customer being identified without controls is low. Having a sanctioned customer could lead to fines and penalties from OFAC, reputational damage, loss of business, and lawsuits from your customer if you cancel a contract. Since there are multiple ways having a sanctioned customer can cause a loss to WeExport, the severity is assessed at the highest level, which is critical.		

Assessing Department or Business Unit Risk

Your risk assessment should also evaluate the sanctions risk of individual departments or business units within your company. This helps identify which units need the most robust controls. For example, a high-risk business unit solely relying on automated screening may require additional controls (such as a referral process) to reduce risk. Or, a foreign unit might need to comply with multiple sanctions regimes.

For each department, evaluate the inherent risk, likelihood, and severity of potential sanctions violations. Later, you'll identify the current sanctions controls the unit relies on, assess those controls, and determine the residual sanctions risk for that business unit. Ideally, this should be part of the unit's individual risk assessment, and you can include these results in the company-wide SRA. However, always review the unit's results and judgments. If a unit believes its sanctions risk is low, but you disagree, that gap must be discussed.

Let's look at an example by analyzing three of WeExport's departments in Table 3. The remainder are included in the completed SRA.

Table 3. Business unit risks of WeExport

Business Unit	Inherent Risk	Likelihood	Severity
Sales - Education	medium-low	unlikely	medium
	Education is a low-risk business unit, as sanctions rarely affect this industry. Therefore, the likelihood of a violation is unlikely and of medium severity should one occur.		
Shipping and Receiving	high	highly likely	critical
	Shipping and receiving are considered high risk because they ship globally, there are many parties to a shipment, goods can be shipped to countries where they are prohibited, and some shipping routes can go through sanctioned jurisdictions. Therefore, the likelihood is high that a sanctions violation would occur without controls and that the severity of the penalty would have a critical impact on the company.		
Procurement	medium-high	likely	high
	Procurement is considered a higher-risk area since they are responsible for identifying, contracting with, and monitoring third parties with whom WeExport does business. The number of third parties is not high, and most are not in high-risk areas, lowering inherent risk slightly. However, several of these third parties are located in foreign countries. Therefore, the likelihood of a violation absent any controls is likely with a high severity of impact.		

What Countries Are Higher Risk

You might be wondering how to identify which countries pose higher risks. There are several methods to consider, and a country that ends up being rated high risk according to one or more of these methods should be regarded as high risk:

- Countries with OFAC sanctions programs[73] should be considered higher risk. Those countries with trade embargoes—Iran, Syria, Cuba, North Korea, and Russian-held regions of Ukraine, such as Crimea—are the highest risk since most business activity in those countries is prohibited. Also, consider countries that are allied with these highest-risk countries. For example, China and India are two countries that are friendly toward Russia. Even though India doesn't have a sanctions program, it may be considered at increased risk compared to a country such as the UK.
- The Financial Action Task Force (FATF)[74] lists countries on "black" and "gray" lists for anti-money laundering deficiencies. These countries can be considered high-risk due to their lack of controls over fraud and abuse. Currently, Iran, Myanmar, and North Korea are on the black list.
- Transparency International[75] is a great resource that calculates a corruption index and ranks countries based on their level of corruption. Download their Corruption Perceptions Index spreadsheet to identify if a country you are doing business in is considered corrupt. According to their 2024 index, the least corrupt country is Denmark; the most corrupt country is South Sudan.
- Current events should also factor into your geographic risk analysis. While there are no sanctions programs over Israel, the fact it is a current political hot spot should move it toward the top of your risk list if you do business there.
- As mentioned, some areas of the US are considered higher risk than others. This may help organizations that only operate domestically to assess their geographical risk. These jurisdictions can be determined using the maps of the High Intensity Drug Trafficking Area (HIDTA)[76] and High Intensity Financial Crimes Area (HIFCA).[77] Customers located in these areas are generally considered at increased risk.

You will notice we didn't assess residual risk in this chapter. Residual risk will be evaluated once the controls are identified and assessed. The next chapter discusses identifying and assessing the controls to help mitigate all the sanctions risks you've identified.

24

Identify Controls

Ensuring you have the proper controls to adequately address the risks identified in your analysis is crucial for your program's success. Without appropriate and effective safeguards, your program will not succeed, and your company could face fines and penalties. If you are just starting to develop the sanctions program, you might not have any controls yet. Or controls might be scattered throughout the company.

What Are Controls

Internal controls are the processes, procedures, and measures that prevent and detect sanctions violations. Internal controls will reduce your sanctions risks. You may have a good idea of what controls exist within the company from the scoping phase of the SRA.

If you have a risk where you can't identify a mitigating control, you have a control gap that must be resolved. This will be discussed in a later chapter.

What Controls Should Be Implemented

Your controls will vary depending on your industry, size, and global scope. However, these are some of the critical controls you will want to implement:

- a written sanctions program—Chapter 6
- an economic sanctions policy—Chapter 8
- program oversight—Chapter 7
- automated scanning/screening of customers and transactions—Chapter 10
- customer due diligence—Chapter 11
- third party due diligence—Chapter 11
- training—Chapter 14
- contract language—Chapter 12
- risk assessment—Chapter 16
- auditing and testing—Chapter 15
- written procedures—Chapter 9
- environmental scanning—Chapter 13

If these sound familiar, it's because earlier chapters explained why they're key to a strong sanctions program. Those chapters also covered how to implement these controls effectively. If any are missing, it creates a weak spot in your program called a **control gap**.

In your risk assessment, note which team or department performs the control. Including a contact person in the department for any follow-up questions is helpful.

Third Parties and Controls

A control that an external party performs for you is not a control for your program. You can't depend solely on an external third party, like a bank, to carry out a control for you. Instead, you must either (1) perform the control yourself (such as screening a payee before sending a payment to the bank) or (2) oversee the third party's completion of the control procedure.

For example, as part of your compliance testing program, you might periodically audit payments issued by a vendor to ensure they are being screened appropriately. While you can acknowledge in the risk assessment that a third party performs a control, your company's control is overseeing the vendor's actions. OFAC doesn't permit a company to rely solely on a third party to fulfill its sanctions requirements without oversight.[78]

Technology Is Key

Remember those "adequate resources" senior management is expected to provide to the sanctions compliance function? A sanctions compliance program will not be effective by relying only on manual controls. People make mistakes, and manual work requires more staff. That's why automated procedures and applications are essential tools for sanctions compliance. Some processes that may require automation to be an effective control include:
- Scanning System - This is the number one technology a sanctions compliance program needs. See Chapter 10 for more information on how to vet a screening application for purchase.
- Environmental Scanning - While a spreadsheet will work to document the environmental scan process for smaller companies, a risk

management system, such as Archer (https://www.archerirm.com/), which we used, would work better for larger companies.
- Risk Assessment - While a spreadsheet will work to document the risk assessment process for smaller companies, a risk management system, such as Archer, which we used, would work better for larger companies.
- Training Platform - An automated training platform (i.e., a learning management system) can maintain your sanctions training course, update it easily, automatically roll it out to large groups, and track who has completed it and when. Smaller companies may be able to do this manually, however, if needed.
- Document Management System - Nowadays, most documents and emails are kept digitally rather than on paper. A document management system is beneficial because it can automatically store documents securely, making them easy for anyone in the company to find and retrieve. These systems also automatically back up the documents to ensure their safety. Sanctions-related documents need to be retained for ten years.

Case Study: Controls for WeExport

Table 4 contains examples of controls identified for WeExport for the sanctions risks.

Table 4. Controls for WeExport

Sanctions Risk	Controls
The company does not identify sanctions issues.	Documented sanctions program approved by the chief compliance officer. The company has a team dedicated to sanctions compliance.
Sanctioned customers are not identified.	Customers are screened at onboarding and periodically thereafter using an automated system. Customer due diligence is conducted at account opening.

Table 4 (continued).

Sanctions Risk	Controls
Transactions that violate sanctions are conducted.	OFAC watchlist screening of all payment transactions using an automated system. Accounts Payable manually scans all wire payments before their release to the bank.
Employees don't understand sanctions or follow sanctions procedures.	Annual training is required for sanctions compliance staff.
New sanctions requirements are not identified and implemented.	Environmental scanning identifies new sanctions requirements.
Third parties may put the company at risk for sanctions violations	Vendor due diligence is conducted at onboarding Contract provisions prohibit certain activities by vendors, wholesalers, and other third parties doing business on the company's behalf.

25

Assess Controls

Once you've identified all applicable sanctions-related controls, you should assess their effectiveness and sufficiency.

Control Effectiveness

Effectiveness asks if the control functions properly. Does it work consistently, occasionally, or not at all? Or is there no control in place?

A control can be evaluated as "effective," "partially effective," or "ineffective." A partially effective control is in place and somewhat functional, but there may be a gap. For instance, the claims team might manually scan many, but not all, payments before sending them out. Or, you may scan some, but not all parties, against sanctions watchlists.

An ineffective control isn't performed or doesn't work more often than not. For example, sanctions training has never been provided to staff.

Residual Risk

You can assess the residual risk of your sanctions risks now that the controls and their effectiveness are identified. As a reminder, residual risk is the likelihood—high, medium, or low—that a sanctions violation will occur after the controls are performed. The residual risk will tell you if your controls are sufficient to mitigate the sanctions risk, if additional controls are needed, or if controls need to be revised.

Obviously, the inherent risk will not change if you have no controls to mitigate a risk. A partially effective control may only slightly reduce the risk (moving it from high to medium-high) or may not reduce the risk at all.

You should reassess residual risk after strengthening these controls or implementing new ones to plug gaps.

Remember, a risk is only reduced if the control is in place, working, and completely mitigates the risk.

Control Sufficiency

After assessing the residual risk, you know whether the control indeed reduced the risk, even if it works effectively. This is considered control sufficiency.

For example, suppose you scan all payments through your automated system, with the data being processed overnight. You verify that the system and scanning are working correctly. This control seems effective at reducing the risk of paying a sanctioned party. However, when you look closer, you find that wire payments are sent to the bank and processed during the day before the overnight scan. So, a payment could be issued to an SDN before the match is identified through scanning. Therefore, this control isn't entirely sufficient because not all transactions are scanned before they are issued.

Additional Control Measures

You may also want to consider other aspects of your controls, such as whether they are automated, manual, preventative, or detective. Here's what these terms mean:

- **Automated controls** are performed without human intervention. For example, the scanning control is automated if you have a sanctions screening application.
- **Manual controls** require a person to perform them. If accounts payable manually scans payee names before sending a wire transfer, that's a manual process.

A control can have both automated and manual elements. For instance, your scanning control might use an automated system, but a person has to manually review any potential matches it generates.

- **Preventative controls** stop a sanctions violation from occurring if performed correctly. For example, if your sanctions screening system automatically stops a payment to a sanctioned party, that's a preventative control.
- **Detective controls** identify a sanctions issue after it has occurred, giving you time to correct it before it becomes a violation. For

example, a manager may review a new account before onboarding to ensure all due diligence steps are performed.

A control can have a preventative and detective element, although that is less likely.

This analysis helps you assess the strength of your controls. If your entire program relies on manual detective controls, it's weaker because human error can occur. Manual controls are more prone to mistakes and might not always be performed. Detective controls don't prevent errors from happening in the first place. If a detective control fails, no backup prevents a violation.

A more robust program relies primarily on automated, preventative controls. These don't require human intervention or judgment, and they stop violations from occurring right away.

Case Study: Control Assessment for WeExport

Table 5 is the assessment for a sample of controls identified for WeExport. A more complete analysis can be found in the completed SRA.

Table 5. Controls assessment for WeExport

Sanctions risk	Control	Risk & Controls Analysis	
Transactions that violate sanctions are conducted.	Accounts payable manually screens all wire payments before their release to the bank.	Manual control	The accounts payable staff must manually scan the payee's name, as once the payment is sent to the bank, it is automatically released before the nightly automated scan of payments occurs.
		Preventative control	The payee's name is scanned before the wire is released to the bank to be sent.
Inherent risk: medium-high		Risk score	Partially effective. Staff do not consistently scan wire payments before releasing them to the bank.
Residual risk: medium		Most payments are automatically scanned by the system, which reduces residual risk. However, not all wire payments are checked before being released to the bank.	

Table 5 (continued).

Sanctions Risk	Control		Risk & Controls Analysis
Employees don't understand sanctions or follow sanctions procedures.	Annual training is required for sanctions compliance staff.	Manual control	Sanctions compliance staff identify and attend training through outside organizations.
		Preventative controls	Training helps provide employees with knowledge that will assist them in complying with sanctions regulations. It does not detect a lack of staff knowledge of sanctions.
Inherent risk: high		Risk score	Ineffective. Most staff at WeExport who perform sanctions-related controls have received no sanctions training in the last three years.
Residual risk: high			Control is ineffective, so inherent risk remains unchanged.
Third parties may put the company at risk for sanctions violations.	Vendor due diligence is conducted at onboarding.	Manual control	Information on the potential vendor is obtained and reviewed manually.
		Preventative control	Due diligence is conducted before contracting with a new third party, which helps prevent a risky third party from becoming a contractor.
Inherent risk: medium-high		Risk score	Partially effective. While due diligence before onboarding is considered adequate, there is no ongoing monitoring of vendors for new sanctions issues during the contract term.
Residual risk: medium			Residual risk drops slightly to medium due to initial due diligence and scanning of third-party payments.

As you can see from the analysis in Table 5, there are instances where the controls aren't working as effectively as expected or don't exist. The next chapter will explore what to do next.

26

Gap Identification and Remediation

Now that you've identified and assessed the sanctions controls in place, you've arrived at the critical part of the risk assessment: What are your control gaps, why do those gaps exist (i.e., the root cause), and what can you do to close those gaps?

Control Gaps

A control gap happens when the controls don't operate well or are missing altogether. You have a control gap if:
- you have a sanctions risk with no control to mitigate it
- your control isn't functioning effectively
- your control does not adequately cover the risk (sufficiency)
- you have an inherent risk that hasn't been reduced by the control in place

Root Cause Analysis

The first step to remedy this gap is to figure out why it happened. You may hear this referred to as a "root cause analysis," as it means getting to the primary or "root" reason why a control deficiency occurred so you can implement an appropriate solution.

Perhaps procedures are outdated, technology is insufficient, resources are inadequate to perform the tasks, or the procedure got dropped when a function was reorganized. All of those can be reasons why a control gap exists.

To conduct the analysis, just ask "why?" A common root cause methodology is the Five Why's approach, which means asking "why?" five times to get to the root cause.[79] But you don't need to ask exactly five questions; some issues may be identified quicker or require more research.

Let's conduct an example root cause analysis using WeExport.

In WeExport's risk assessment, they learned that employees weren't consistently manually scanning payees before sending a wire to the bank. The control is manually screening payees; the gap is that it isn't being performed. When you ask why, you learn it's because employees didn't know they were supposed to. When you again ask why, you discover they haven't been trained on the procedure. In fact, no one has trained employees on sanctions for at least three years, and they don't understand them. This is the root cause of the problem.

Remediation

The last step is to close the gap by redesigning the control or implementing a new one. Document the control gaps in your risk assessment and create a plan to fix them.

Obtain support from senior management for any new procedures. Use your risk assessment to show management that these controls are necessary to avoid serious consequences. Sometimes, fixing these issues may cost money, which will need approval. This expense might need to be added to next year's budget instead of being fixed immediately.

Collaborate on the new or revised procedures with those responsible for carrying them out. When you create procedures solely based on your vision, they may not be feasible for the staff tasked with implementing them, and they will push back on doing them or not do them at all. Engage with the team from the start; they often have valuable insights on executing the procedures effectively. This approach ensures their initial support for the procedure and increases the likelihood of its success.

Once you've fixed the control gaps, reassess the new and revised controls to ensure they work effectively. Reassess the residual risk to verify that the sanctions risk has decreased due to the new controls. Schedule the reassessment one to three months in the future to allow time for the controls to work and to gather data on their effectiveness.

There may be situations where a control gap exists, but remediating the issue would be too costly or burdensome. If the inherent risk for a sanctions risk is not high, the line of business may accept the risk. This means management is aware of the gap and has decided not to remediate it. The reason for acceptance should be well documented, should it ever become an issue in court or with OFAC.

Case Study: Control Gaps and Remediation for WeExport

Table 6 assesses a sample of the control gaps identified for WeExport. The remainder can be found in the completed SRA.

Table 6. Control gaps and remediation for WeExport

Control	Control Gap	Remediation Plan
Customer due diligence is conducted at account opening.	There is no review of beneficial ownership.	WeExport will conduct a project to strengthen the customer due diligence process, including developing a method to identify and scan beneficial owners of certain types of customers and reviewing third-party databases of beneficial ownership information to determine if one would be suitable and cost-effective.
Accounts payable manually screens all wire payments before their release to the bank.	Accounts payable staff do not consistently scan wire payments before releasing them to the bank.	Training specific to how and when to complete the manual scan of payees will be created and issued by the end of the year.
Annual training is required for sanctions compliance staff.	Most staff at WeExport have received no sanctions training in the last three years, including staff that perform sanctions-related controls.	A basic sanctions training program will be developed and issued to all employees in the company.
Environmental scanning identifies new sanctions requirements.	Environmental scan tracking is conducted manually via a spreadsheet. An automated system would be stronger.	None. Management accepts this minor risk. While an automated system would be better for tracking new regulations and their implementation within the company, the cost of a risk management system is prohibitive at this time.

27

Risk Assessment Documentation and Next Steps

The final results of your risk assessment should be documented using a spreadsheet or Word document, such as the one provided with this guide. Here, again, is the link to download the risk assessment template, plus the final example risk assessment for WeExport: https://easysanctions.wordpress.com/the-plain-english-guide-to-economic-sanctions-risk-assessments/. A risk management system, such as Archer (https://www.archerirm.com/), used at my prior organization, would work better for larger companies.

Generally, the company's sanctions compliance officer should share the completed risk assessment with senior management, such as the chief compliance officer, get their approval for any necessary fixes, and keep them informed about the progress of gap remediation. Ongoing discussions should be held between sanctions compliance and senior management regarding changes in the risk profile.

The progress of gap remediation does not need to be included in the risk assessment but would usually be documented in project plans, progress memos, and related documents.

A risk assessment should be considered a "living document," meaning it should be reviewed and updated regularly or when a significant change occurs. This might be when new sanctions arise, your company's profile changes (like buying a foreign subsidiary or opening a new foreign manufacturing facility), or new controls are implemented (for example, when a new automated system is installed). At my prior firm, we revised the risk assessment when we purchased a foreign entity and revised it again when Russia invaded Ukraine.

The SRA should be reviewed and updated at least annually in any case.

Training should be held on various sanctions topics based on the results of your risk assessment. This ongoing education ensures everyone stays informed and compliant with the latest sanctions regulations and procedures.

Ongoing oversight and controls testing should be conducted to ensure there are no changes to their assessment in your SRA.

HOW TO HANDLE SANCTIONED PARTIES AND TRANSACTIONS

28
What if My Customer Is Sanctioned?

What you need to do if your customer is sanctioned depends on a few factors: whether they are a current or prospective customer, if you hold any assets for them, and which sanctions program they fall under. Some programs restrict only specific activities, not all.

Don't Do Business with Them

For most programs, this will be the first requirement. This means you cannot open an account, issue a policy, sign a contract to provide goods or services, or process a transaction for a party named on the SDN list.

If you already have an account open or active business with them, you must stop working with them immediately. When someone is sanctioned under a blocking program, you can no longer provide any services to them, including activities that would wind down the business, unless a license is issued (licenses are discussed in the next chapter). These assets will sit there until they expire (in the case of a contract or policy) or get frozen (such as an account with funds in it).

Freeze or Block Assets

When a party is sanctioned under a program requiring an asset freeze, you cannot accept payments or assets from them, make payments to them, or provide other economic resources (such as loans) to them as of the date they are added to the list. In theory, OFAC considers any asset owned by a sanctioned party (including cars, townhomes, etc.) to be blocked and cannot be dealt with.

If the asset belongs to the Specially Designated National (SDN), you can't reject the transaction; you must block the assets. Some examples of how this works follow:
- If you receive a loan payment on an account belonging to an SDN, you must retain and block those funds. You can't return them, nor can you apply the payment to their loan balance.

- If you have a payment due to an SDN on a valid insurance claim, again, you can't send the payment, nor can you deny the claim. The claim payment is considered their asset, and you must block it.
- If you are custodian of an asset belonging to an SDN, such as artwork, you cannot return it.
- If your company holds an insurance policy for an SDN, you can't service it, not even to cancel it.

You will see the terms "blocked" or "frozen" used interchangeably, and they mean the same thing: you cannot release those assets to the SDN.[80] Generally, funds must be put into a bank account blocked by a bank. The account must be interest-bearing, likely prohibiting your company from maintaining the funds in a separate internal account. Maintaining the funds in an internal account and "imputing" interest (i.e., calculating the amount of interest the SDN would receive if the funds were in a bank account) is also inappropriate.

Once the funds are in this blocked bank account, neither you nor the sanctioned party can access them without permission from OFAC. However, the title to the assets remains with the SDN.[81] It is best to contact OFAC for guidance on blocking assets the first time.

Insurance Company Policy Blocking

Blocking assets for an insurance company is a bit more complicated than for a bank blocking an account. OFAC expects you to "block" a policy as it's considered an asset, and we did that in my prior position. You are not required to move the policy to a blocked bank account as you would if you held funds, but you will need to work with the line of business to ensure no further activity is performed on the account until the policy expires. If there is a wind-down license, you can try to cancel the policy during the license term if there is sufficient time.

If you receive premium payments after the time of the sanction (some customers may try to keep a policy active, thinking the sanction will soon be removed), you will need to block those funds unless there is a wind-down license that allows receiving and returning the funds. Without a wind-down license, you can't return them to the sanctioned party, nor can you apply the payment to their policy.

Nuances for Foreign Companies Blocking Assets Under OFAC

For foreign companies, you should note that OFAC only requires blocking of assets that are present in the US when blocked, enter the US once blocked, or that are in the possession or control of any US person. For example, if a foreign branch of a US company holds assets belonging to an SDN, it is considered a US person and would need to block them.

Also, if a foreign insurance company has an insurance policy with a US nexus, and the insured gets sanctioned by OFAC, the policy is considered a blocked asset. No claims can be paid under it to any party, even a non-sanctioned party.

On the other hand, if you are a foreign person dealing with an OFAC-sanctioned person or entity, and there is no US nexus—meaning no US persons, entities, currency, goods, or financial institutions are involved—then OFAC regulations do not require you to block their assets. But be certain secondary sanctions don't apply, or you will need to freeze the asset.

Reject a Transaction

In some sanctions programs, the requirement is not to freeze assets but to prohibit the transaction altogether. Some examples of when you would reject a transaction and not freeze the asset include:
- A bank might reject a money transfer to a country like Iran, which is under comprehensive sanctions since such transactions are forbidden. However, assets are not frozen unless they belong to an SDN.
- A company sends money for a non-sanctioned customer to a sanctioned bank. In this case, the bank's status as an SDN means the transaction should be rejected, but no assets are frozen as the customer is not sanctioned.
- If a prohibited good, like sonar equipment, is being sent to a non-SDN entity in a sanctioned country, you would reject the transaction rather than "freeze" the item.

Insurance-Specific Issues with Claims

Knowing whether to block or reject a claim submitted under a blocked policy can be complex and depends on who the payment is going to.

You must block the proceeds of a valid claim owed to an SDN under a blocked policy, as it is considered the asset of the sanctioned party. Again, you can't send the payment or deny the claim. If the claim is invalid and denied, you don't need to block anything, as there is no asset to block. If you haven't yet reviewed the claim to determine if payment is due, you must pause the process and hold off on further evaluation.

OFAC also does not allow the processing and payment of valid claims for non-sanctioned parties under a frozen policy. The claim, if valid, will need to sit open until such time the payment can be made or a specific license is requested to pay it.[82] This policy differs from the UK and the EU, which allow processing payments to non-sanctioned parties on a claim where the insured is sanctioned, as they don't technically require policies to be "blocked." However, you still cannot pay these claims if there is a US nexus.

In some situations, an insurance company will have a valid claim to a non-sanctioned beneficiary in a comprehensively sanctioned country. This happened to us occasionally for life insurance claims. We had beneficiaries in Iran and Syria who were not sanctioned, and the claims were valid. The claim has to be paid within a certain time period if it's a valid claim. So, is there another way to legally disburse the funds so the beneficiary can receive them?

For the Iranian beneficiary, her daughter in Canada held Power of Attorney. We could legally send her the funds, and she could lawfully send them to her mother under a personal remittance general license (discussed in the next chapter).

We could not find any way to get the Syrian beneficiary the funds, so they had to be escheated to the state. If the beneficiary ever comes to the US, they could gain access to the funds. You can't distribute the funds to the executor (if they are not a family member) or an attorney acting on behalf of the estate, as they cannot take advantage of the personal remittance general license. Nor can you put the funds in a blocked bank account, as the beneficiary is not an SDN.

Note that beneficiaries in Cuba, whether they are SDNs or not, must have their proceeds put in a blocked bank account first. Then, they can petition to have the funds released to someone in the US who can forward them to Cuba via the personal remittance exception.

Report to OFAC

Any time you block assets or reject a transaction due to sanctions, you must file a report within ten business days of the blocking or rejection.[83] There can occasionally be some confusion about when the ten-day clock starts, but we used the date the transaction was completed (e.g., the blocked funds entered the blocked bank account), not when the transaction that needed blocking or rejection was initially identified. You can file online at https://ofac.treasury.gov/ofac-reporting-system. Again, it is best to contact OFAC for guidance your first time.

If your company holds blocked assets in a blocked bank account, there is an annual requirement (to be filed by September 30) to report those assets to OFAC. Our bank, which held blocked assets for many different entities, filed the annual report for all its blocked accounts, including ours.

Different countries have different reporting requirements. For example, if you have a match to a US and UK SDN and block assets, you will need to report to both governmental entities. The UK also has an annual reporting requirement.

Case Studies

Let's look at two examples of how this would work.

Bob's Bullets is a company that sells ammunition. Bob's Bullets becomes an SDN under OFAC's weapons proliferation sanctions program for selling ammunition to an entity in Iran. An insurance company will no longer be able to provide insurance to Bob's Bullets, such as workers' compensation or property coverage. Banks will no longer be able to maintain accounts or process transactions for Bob's Bullets. No matter what your business is (for example, if you rent Bob's Bullets their manufacturing facility), you will no longer be able to provide that service. Any assets these companies have belonging to Bob's Bullets, such as an insurance policy, a pending claims payment, a bank account, or a rent payment, now must be frozen by the holder. Once they block those assets, each entity will file a report to OFAC notifying them of the assets being held.

The second example assumes you are a foreign company.

You are a German-based company that produces computer chips that contain US parts. These parts give you a US nexus for any transactions related to these chips.

John's Tech is a Canadian company that uses those chips in the computers it builds. John's Tech becomes an OFAC SDN under a blocking program for selling technology to an entity in Iran.

You cannot sell computer chips to John's Tech as they contain US parts (the US nexus) and OFAC sanctioned John's Tech.

You cannot use a third party (such as a wholesaler) in another country to sell John's Tech the chips. Again, they contain US parts and retain their US nexus even in another country. OFAC would consider you to be selling the chips indirectly to John's Tech.

You cannot arrange to sell the chips to one of the owners of John's Tech, who is not sanctioned. This is considered facilitation and is an OFAC violation.

If John's Tech has already sent you payment for the chips, that money must be blocked. The payment cannot be returned to John's Tech since he is sanctioned under a blocking program. You cannot deposit them into your operating account. They must be deposited into a blocked bank account and reported to OFAC.

Your insurance company cannot provide insurance related to any transactions with John's Tech (such as coverage during shipment). Your bank cannot receive funds or send payments to John's Tech.

You cannot purchase any computers from John's Tech as they may contain US-origin parts.

29
Can I Do Any Business with Sanctioned Parties or Countries?

Even when sanctions are in place against certain parties and countries, OFAC provides legal ways to do business with these parties. They do this through licenses or a non-prohibited transaction.

What Is a License?

A license is permission from OFAC to conduct business normally prohibited by a sanction. There are two types of licenses: general and specific.

OFAC has established general licenses that anyone can use for certain transactions. Sometimes, you can conduct your business under a general license.

If no general license is available, you must apply to OFAC for a specific license.[84] A specific license is permission granted by OFAC to a specific party for a particular transaction. Let's take a closer look at these licenses.

General Licenses

OFAC general licenses are available to anyone who believes their activities fit within the terms of the license. You don't need to ask OFAC for permission to use one, and you don't have to tell them you are using it. You can find these licenses on the sanctions program pages under "General Licenses" or in the CFR. General licenses issued outside of the CFR can expire, renew, or be canceled before they expire, but those in the CFR generally don't.

Some general licenses are called "wind-down licenses." They let you keep doing business with a newly sanctioned party briefly while you wrap up your dealings with them. They do not allow you to continue business as usual.

Some activities are licensed under a general license for multiple programs, such as those that cover legal services, work of the US government or international organizations such as the Red Cross, telecommunications, internet communications, and protecting intellectual property like patents and trademarks.

Jurisdictions such as the UK and the EU also issue general licenses that allow certain activities despite sanctions. However, don't assume that because one country has a general license, another country also allows the same activity under their general license. Also, the UK can require companies to report when using a general license, which OFAC does not.

Below is a discussion of a couple of the more commonly used general licenses.

Humanitarian Aid

The US generally does not prohibit transactions related to humanitarian aid under its sanctions programs, even for countries with trade embargoes.[85]

OFAC has issued general licenses allowing these transactions in most programs, as well as guidance on how to comply with them.

So, what is considered humanitarian aid?

Generally, these transactions are linked to agriculture, food, medicine, medical devices, and replacement parts. It can also include activities conducted by nonprofit groups that work toward public and social welfare goals or international organizations that benefit the civilian population by meeting basic human needs or building democracy, such as the United Nations World Food Programme.

It is crucial to remember just because someone says a transaction is for humanitarian reasons, don't rely on it. Not everything fits the definition of humanitarian aid in the sanctions regulations. For instance, some pesticides (generally allowed under the agricultural general license) can't be sent to certain countries, like Russia, because they might be used for chemical weapons. Also, some medical devices need a specific license to export.[86] Plus, these humanitarian licenses usually don't let you transfer funds to a sanctioned party. Always ensure the transaction or good is covered under the humanitarian license for that program.

Other jurisdictions, such as the UK and the EU, also have humanitarian exceptions in their sanctions programs. However, don't assume the humanitarian licenses allow the same activity among all the jurisdictions.

Personal Remittances

Comprehensive sanctions programs, such as those for Iran, Syria, Cuba, North Korea, and Crimea, permit US individuals to send non-commercial, personal remittances to these countries.[87] General licenses enable financial institutions to process these transactions. With a personal remittance general license, individuals can send money to close relatives in a comprehensively sanctioned area.

However, if the transaction is commercial (e.g., making a purchase or paying an insurance claim), this general license doesn't apply.

For instance, Antonio can send money to his aunt in Cuba without violating US rules. His bank can also process the transfer.

But if Antonio were to die and leave his aunt in Cuba the proceeds of his life insurance policy, the payment of the claim to the aunt would be considered a commercial transaction by the insurance company, and the insurer can't use the personal remittance general license to send the funds.

Specific License

A specific license is a written document granted by OFAC to one party for permission to conduct a transaction or series of transactions that would otherwise be prohibited by sanctions.[88] The party who wants a specific license has to apply for it, and OFAC may or may not approve it. Plus, it can take a long time to get one approved. Only parties covered under the specific license can use it.

When applying for the license, request coverage for all third parties involved in the transaction. This could include insurance companies handling claims, third-party providers hired for assistance, and banks handling payments. Otherwise, each organization involved in the transaction may need a separate license to participate. Just because someone you are doing business with has a license doesn't mean your company does unless you are listed in the license.

In addition, having a Bureau of Industry and Security (BIS) license to export a specific good doesn't eliminate the need for an OFAC license if OFAC otherwise prohibits the transaction. Likewise, if you have an OFAC license for the good, be aware that you may or may not also need a BIS license to export it.

In my prior position, we used specific licenses to make payments on claims that would otherwise be prohibited due to sanctions. For example, a maritime incident occurred in Crimean waters, a comprehensively sanctioned jurisdiction. The general license allowed the issuance of claims payments and the hiring of third parties to conduct salvage, among other services. We also applied for a license to pay claims to non-sanctioned third parties (such as a loss adjustor) under a blocked policy.

You can also apply for a specific license to maintain a policy, such as when a sanctioned parent company owns a US-based company. This was the case when Russia's Rusal was sanctioned. Since Rusal America, their US subsidiary, was also considered sanctioned under the 50 Percent Rule, you could apply for a license to keep doing business with them.

Non-Prohibited Transactions

As mentioned before, depending on the program someone is sanctioned under, you may still be able to do business with them, just not the prohibited activity. This occurs most with parties sanctioned under Non-SDN list programs. If you identify a customer or other party as a positive match, review the program under which they are sanctioned to see what is prohibited.

For example, suppose you want to purchase a product from a company in China. You search the OFAC list and find out they are sanctioned under the Non-SDN Chinese Military-Industrial Complex Companies List. This program prohibits the purchase of public securities of certain Chinese companies due to their ties to the Chinese military. However, it allows other types of transactions, such as purchasing goods.[89] In this example, you can proceed with your transaction, as the prohibitions of this sanctions program do not apply to your purchase.

Our company had a Hong Kong office with many Chinese customers, some of whom were on this list. However, the insurance we provided was not considered the purchase of public securities, so we could offer the insurance.

Whether you want to do business with this company is another matter. Your organization's reputational risk is a fair consideration when deciding to provide any services, even allowed transactions, to someone on one of OFAC's watchlists.

Guidance and Frequently Asked Questions (FAQs)

I've discussed reviewing different sources, such as Executive Orders, Directives, general licenses, and the CFR, to see if you can do business with someone. Two additional sources to review that may assist you in deciding if your transaction is allowed are guidance and FAQs.

OFAC sometimes issues guidance on topics like complying with humanitarian general licenses and providing legal help to sanctioned parties. They have also issued over one thousand FAQs that answer common questions about their rules. These FAQs cover everything from what OFAC does to specifics about what you can and can't do under different sanctions programs or with newly sanctioned parties.

But remember, guidance and FAQs are not the same as licenses or regulations; they don't have the force of law. Instead, they are more like this guide, helping you understand and comply with sanctions. Interpretations can and do change over time, so staying updated and consulting with internal or external legal counsel when needed is essential.

If you encounter a situation where your customer is sanctioned, or a transaction you are trying to conduct appears prohibited, review the program to see if the activity is allowed under the sanction or if there is a general license. If not, consider whether the transaction is important enough to apply to OFAC for a specific license. If you need additional insight, consult OFAC's guidance and FAQs to see if they address your specific situation.

OTHER SANCTIONS CONSIDERATIONS

30

Documentation

You may have noticed a theme in this guide: every part of your sanctions compliance program must be documented. This helps you keep track of decisions you made, controls you implemented, how alerts were cleared, what training was provided, etc., and goes a long way toward showing OFAC you have an effective program if there is a possible sanctions violation.

OFAC previously recommended keeping documentation for five years[90], but that requirement is changing to ten years starting March 15, 2025.[91] If your company has been following the five-year rule, now is the time to inform affected staff (including those in other business units) to prevent premature document purging. Larger companies should also update their company-wide document retention policies to reflect this change. Some documents, like those related to blocked property, may need to be kept indefinitely, as you may need to refer to them occasionally.

If you don't have a document management system, ensure your documents are stored on a server accessible to everyone and regularly backed up, with backups stored offsite or in the cloud when possible.

31
What Are the Penalties for Non-Compliance?

OFAC is responsible for civil enforcement of US sanctions laws and regulations. Violations can result in substantial fines, and civil and criminal penalties can exceed several million dollars.[92] Other governmental agencies, such as the Department of Justice (DOJ) or the New York Department of Financial Services, can also impose their own penalties for the same conduct.

Below are a couple larger fines that illustrate the extent to which a company may be subject to penalties.

British American Tobacco (BAT) settled with OFAC for $508 million for violations of the weapons proliferation and North Korea sanctions regulations. BAT is UK-based, and its foreign subsidiary in Singapore was also involved in these transactions, so they aren't automatically US persons for purposes of these regulations. However, the transactions had a US nexus, specifically using a US correspondent banking account and a foreign branch of a US bank to clear these transactions.[93]

The largest fine to date happened in November 2023, totaling $968 million, against Binance. Government agencies such as the Financial Crimes Enforcement Network (FinCEN), Internal Revenue Service (IRS), and Department of Justice (DOJ) were also involved. Binance got in trouble for not setting up systems to spot and report suspicious transactions involving terrorists, ransomware gangs, money launderers, and other criminals. OFAC said Binance purposely undermined and ineffectually implemented its own sanctions compliance controls.[94]

Besides fines, employees, officers, and directors face severe consequences like losing their jobs or going to jail. The DOJ and the US Attorney might bring criminal charges. For instance, in 2022, a US citizen was sentenced to more than five years in prison. He violated sanctions laws by helping North Korea use blockchain and cryptocurrency to hide money and avoid US sanctions.[95]

It is important to note that OFAC operates on a strict liability basis. This means you can be fined for a violation of any amount (in theory, one dollar), even if you did not intend to violate sanctions. However, penalties will depend, in part, on the amount of the violation, whether it was inadvertent or deliberate, and whether you identified and reported the breach to OFAC.

You can significantly lower the fine if you self-report an identified violation to OFAC. OFAC considers non-reporting to be an aggravating factor that could increase your penalty. Binance, for example, did not self-report the violations to OFAC.

And don't overlook the damage to your reputation and your company's reputation when OFAC releases a press statement about your violation. Bad publicity and all the negative fallout from that violation can hurt your finances even more. Banks and other groups might use this negative news to decide whether to work with you.

32
Are Sanctions the Same in Every Country?

We won't go into detail in this guide, but be aware that sanctions regimes differ from country to country, so don't fall into the trap of thinking that if a transaction is legal to conduct in one country, it is okay in another.

Here are some examples of how sanctions rules differ by jurisdiction using a comparison of US sanctions versus EU and UK sanctions:

- The US is the only major economy that has a sanctions program against Cuba.
- The EU and UK have "blocking statutes,"[96] which prevent anyone under EU or UK jurisdiction from following regulations that conflict with their own. As such, they don't allow parties to comply with OFAC sanctions (such as for Iran and Cuba) when they conflict with the EU's and UK's sanctions programs. This was discussed in more detail in Chapter 12.
- The EU and UK have sanctions programs against some countries that the US does not, such as Tunisia and Guinea-Bissau. Therefore, it's essential to ensure you comply with the sanctions for any jurisdiction involved in the transaction, even if it wouldn't violate OFAC rules.
- The EU's and UK's lists of designated parties may differ from OFAC's watchlists and each other's. You should check the watchlists for every jurisdiction in which you do business.
- The EU and the UK may have sanctions programs targeting the same countries as the US, but their restrictions often differ. For example, the UK and the EU have sanctions programs against Venezuela. However, unlike the US, the EU does not ban transactions with the Venezuelan government or Petróleos de Venezuela (PdVSA), the country's largest energy producer. Similarly, while the US has a complete trade embargo against Iran, the UK and the EU have less restrictive sanctions. Their rules mainly focus on exports of goods or technology that could be used in weapons or military applications.
- The 50 Percent Rule applies to ownership *and control* in the EU and the UK, while in the US, it applies only to ownership. When conducting business in the EU or the UK with SDNs who control the

company (including minority owners, executives, or board members), be cautious, as they may be viewed as holding majority control. This can be challenging to determine in practice, so consulting legal counsel is recommended if you encounter this situation. It's also important to note that the UK's 50 percent threshold starts at 50.01 percent ownership, or "more than 50 percent," while the US and EU set it at 50.00 percent or more. This distinction can be significant, as sanctioned parties sometimes reduce their ownership to just below the threshold. For example, if a sanctioned party owns exactly 50.00 percent of a company, that company would be sanctioned under OFAC but not in the UK. Additionally, the UK does not combine ownership stakes among sanctioned parties to determine if an entity meets the 50 Percent Rule unless the rights are under a joint arrangement or one party controls another's rights.

Remember, if you do business outside of the US (sell products, have foreign offices, have foreign customers or vendors), you must also comply with the sanctions regulations in that country—and they may differ from the US's sanctions.

33
Economic Sanctions Nuances

You can see by now that sanctions are not straightforward and are open to interpretation. Here are a few key things to know about sanctions that aren't so obvious in the regulations but are critical to ensuring sanctions compliance.

Foreign Branches Versus Foreign Subsidiaries

Foreign branches are always considered US persons under OFAC regulations. Some large companies have complex ownership structures, so it's essential to trace ownership up the chain to determine if a US person ultimately owns a foreign branch.

Foreign subsidiaries face different sanctions challenges. They are considered US persons for sanctions related to Iran, Cuba, and North Korea, and they might also need to comply with OFAC's secondary sanctions and other situations with a US nexus. It's crucial to understand these nuances and how they could impact business transacted by your subsidiary.

US Territory

US territory isn't just the fifty states and the District of Columbia. It is broadly defined as "United States, its territories and possessions, and all areas under the jurisdiction or authority thereof."[97] For example, American Samoa and Guam are US territories, so they are not considered foreign countries for sanctions. "Areas under the jurisdiction" include places under US control in foreign countries, like military bases and embassies. So, doing business in these areas isn't viewed as occurring on foreign soil. For instance, Guantanamo Bay in Cuba isn't covered by Cuban sanctions because it is technically under US jurisdiction, not Cuba's. If you do business in these areas, you should know that OFAC regulations apply there.

Indirect

OFAC prohibits the direct and indirect provision of prohibited goods or services. Direct is self-explanatory, but what is indirect?

If a company sells goods or services to someone acting on behalf of a sanctioned party or country, even without knowing it, they are indirectly doing business with that sanctioned party. For example, if a firm sells US-made computer parts to a wholesaler in India, who then sells them to customers in Russia or Cuba—where the firm is not allowed to sell directly—the firm is indirectly supplying prohibited goods.

An example is Alfa Laval Middle East, which OFAC fined for causing its US affiliate to export goods from the US to Iran indirectly. They did this by falsely listing a Dubai-based company as the end-user on their export paperwork.[98]

That's why having a clause in your contract that prohibits your goods from being sold in certain sanctioned countries is crucial.

Reinsurance can also be considered indirect provision of services to the customer via a third party (the primary insurer). Reinsurance complexities are discussed further in Chapter 37.

Facilitation

"Facilitation" means helping others break sanctions rules. It could be offering financial help, organizing support, or providing aid that lets sanctioned people, groups, or countries avoid sanctions.[99] You cannot facilitate a transaction that, if you conducted it yourself, would violate OFAC sanctions. OFAC doesn't allow facilitation, and breaking this rule can have severe legal consequences, as it weakens sanctions and supports illegal actions.

Facilitation could be as simple as referring prohibited business to another company not covered by the OFAC regulation. Our organization was concerned that even referring business to our UK subsidiary—when our domestic companies couldn't write those policies—might be considered facilitation, which could violate sanctions rules.

OFAC has fined entities for this type of activity. AL Tank in the US violated Iranian sanctions by referring an Iranian business opportunity to their Middle East affiliate, thereby facilitating a transaction that would have been prohibited if performed by the US entity.[100]

Sanctions Evasion

Sanctions evasion occurs when people try to structure a transaction to get around sanctions. Common evasion tactics include using straw buyers, creating fake companies, transferring assets to non-sanctioned relatives, trading through third countries, hiding the true origin of goods, or setting up new companies in countries not under sanctions.

For instance, say someone's sanctioned under the Lebanon sanctions program, and a company wants to sell them an appliance. The SDN uses a third party to buy it for them. If the selling company knows or should have known through due diligence that a transaction will ultimately benefit a sanctioned person, they could get into big trouble with OFAC.

In another example, if a foreign entity wants to do business with a sanctioned party, it might falsify or omit information regarding the sanctioned party on wire transfers when using a US bank. This is considered sanctions evasion by OFAC.

Non-US persons are also prohibited from causing US persons to knowingly or unknowingly violate US sanctions by engaging in conduct that evades US sanctions, even if they themselves are not directly breaking the law.[101]

One example is when OFAC fined CSE TransTel, a company based in Singapore, for causing sanctions violations. TransTel did business with Iran and helped a non-US financial institution violate sanctions by purposely concealing the origin or destination of US dollar payments destined for Iranian companies.[102]

United Nations (UN) Requirements

As a United Nations member, the US also requires its citizens and businesses to follow UN sanctions. Generally, if you follow OFAC regulations, you're likely also meeting UN sanctions requirements. When screening for OFAC compliance, you should also check the UN's sanctions watchlists.

Globality of Sanctioned Parties

People and entities worldwide can be listed as SDNs under any OFAC program. For example, a program covering Russia does not mean only

Russian entities are sanctioned under it. Parties in India, China, and even Europe can be sanctioned under this program.

Additionally, parties in countries without formal sanctions programs, including the US, can be sanctioned under any program, such as those sanctioned under the narcotics trafficking program. OFAC fined Wells Fargo for not identifying two persons sanctioned under the Foreign Narcotics Kingpin Sanctions Regulations who opened accounts at the bank using US addresses.[103]

If you handle a transaction with a US nexus and aren't checking the names of all parties, wherever located, against OFAC watchlists, you have a gap in your compliance process. This gap could result in an OFAC violation. We had a situation where a broker of one of our policies only scanned the names of policyholders located in sanctioned countries. When we checked the policyholder's name, we discovered they were sanctioned based on Iranian ownership despite not being located in a sanctioned country.

Multiple Jurisdictions May Be Involved

If your company does business globally, you must follow sanctions regimes in every country where you do business, which can result in several jurisdictions for one transaction.

An example of how this works:

You are a company located in the UK with a Swedish subsidiary that wants to sell computer parts to a Russian entity. The computer parts are US-origin, although currently located with a wholesaler in China.

How many jurisdictions do you have to comply with sanctions in?
- The parent company is in the UK, so there is a UK nexus.
- The subsidiary is in Sweden, so there is a Swedish and EU nexus since Sweden is part of the EU.
- The goods are of US origin, so there is a US nexus.
- The goods are in China, so there is a Chinese nexus.
- The customer is in Russia, a high-risk jurisdiction. The policy is subject to US, UK, and EU sanctions programs over Russia, each with subtle differences regarding Russian exports.

Therefore, for one transaction, you may have to comply with US, UK, and EU sanctions, or more, simultaneously!

Don't assume that sanctions restrictions in your country mirror the US's or vice versa. You should review each country's sanctions laws to ensure the transaction does not violate regulations in any jurisdiction.

34

Managing US Parent Versus Foreign Branch or Subsidiary Conflicts

Global companies sometimes face disagreements between their US headquarters and foreign branches or subsidiaries about whether to take on particular business. The US parent company might be cautious about approving legal business for the foreign office which could lead to future sanctions or reputational problems. On the other hand, the foreign office might want to pursue business even if the US parent company believes it could violate sanctions. In its enforcement release for AL Middle East, OFAC said: "Non-US companies should be aware of how their activities might trigger compliance issues with US sanctions, including when they place orders with US affiliates or subsidiaries."[104]

Resolving these conflicts can be challenging due to legal and regulatory barriers and can lead to tension between legal/compliance and foreign business units, especially when the business comes from VIP customers or offers a high income. Executives may push back against compliance advice to reject the business.

So, can these conflicts be resolved or at least managed?

Ultimately, if the company proceeds with business that appears to be prohibited by OFAC, you will need to decide whether to self-report the violation to reduce a future OFAC penalty. They might also choose to write business that you know, based on your deep understanding of current sanctions, will eventually be prohibited—creating more work to unwind later. You will have to monitor that business carefully so you can take action if and when a sanction occurs.

OFAC has fined many companies for violations their foreign subsidiaries or branches incurred, some of which conducted the transaction after the US parent company told them to cease that activity. One example is Black and Decker, which OFAC fined because its Chinese subsidiary exported or tried to export tools to Iran.[105]

The following are two potential solutions we utilized to manage these conflicts.

Risk Decision Matrix

Documenting the decision-making process in a risk decision matrix could be valuable. It shows who in the company is responsible for decisions on sanctions-related issues. My prior organization had one, and we often referred to it during challenging discussions about sanctions issues that arose. Our matrix was simply an Excel spreadsheet with five levels of decision-making depending on the situation.

Tier 1: Business line staff make the decisions. No sanctions issue exists, so the employees conduct business as usual.

Tier 2: The sanctions compliance team makes the decision. Someone on the sanctions team can resolve a potential sanctions issue, such as clearing a false positive match.

Tier 3: The SCO or the sanctions compliance team manager decides. Potential business that may violate sanctions is escalated to the manager or SCO. They can decline the business if a transaction or account violates sanctions. Otherwise, if necessary, they can resolve the issue with input from other company staff.

Tier 4: Business line management makes the decision. Usually, these decisions are risk-related. The customer or transaction is at high risk for a potential sanctions violation, so the decision is whether to accept the customer or conduct the transaction. Business line management has the final say, although the SCO and legal counsel may provide their input during decision-making. This tier is not for transactions that clearly violate sanctions; that decision rests in Tier 3 with sanctions compliance staff.

Tier 5: Senior management participates in the decision. A sanctions violation may have occurred, so executive management determines the response (such as self-reporting to OFAC) with input from the SCO, legal counsel, and business line staff.

Recusal Policy

Another way to manage these conflicts is by implementing an internal recusal policy. If your foreign subsidiary is legally allowed to do business that your US entity cannot, the transaction may be able to proceed as long as all US involvement is avoided, including any participation from US staff (i.e., a US nexus is avoided).

For example, your foreign subsidiary has an opportunity to write a policy that involves the Venezuelan government, an OFAC-sanctioned group. If there is no other US nexus (no US parties involved in the policy, it's not denominated in US dollars, and transactions don't include US financial institutions, for example), then the business may be allowable if a recusal policy is followed.

We established a recusal policy where US employees, such as underwriters, claims adjusters, and their managers, were excluded from participating in specific policies and claims throughout their duration. The business requiring recusal was identified after a referral to the sanctions compliance team for review, which then informed the foreign subsidiary that US employees couldn't participate in that policy or claim.

However, this won't work in situations involving Iran or Cuba since foreign subsidiaries are US persons under those regulations.

One exception to recusal is that US employees can still offer legal and compliance advice to their foreign counterparts on complying with US sanctions and whether OFAC prohibits a transaction.[106]

If you institute a recusal policy, be careful that no US person gets involved in negotiating, handling, or decision-making on the activity. OFAC fined one company because US senior managers approved contracts for a foreign subsidiary, violating Directive 4 of the Ukraine-/Russia-related Sanctions.[107] This fine may not have occurred if a recusal policy had been properly followed.

35
Trade Sanctions

Foreign companies importing or exporting US-origin goods must consider requirements from two additional agencies beyond OFAC: the Bureau of Industry and Security (BIS) and the Department of State (DoS). While OFAC enforces import and export restrictions on certain countries and individuals, BIS and the DoS focus on licensing specific items, mainly dual-use, military, and defense products. They also maintain lists of restricted parties who cannot sell or receive these goods.

Although BIS and DoS primarily require licenses for sensitive items, their controls are intended to prevent these goods from aiding foreign military and defense sectors. OFAC's trade sanctions, in contrast, cover a broader range, prohibiting many kinds of import/export transactions with specific countries and individuals, some of which overlap the BIS and DoS oversight. Businesses often need to comply with all three agencies.

For foreign companies dealing with countries under OFAC's import/export sanctions, it's essential to ensure that products don't contain US-origin parts or weren't made in the US, as this could lead to violations of both OFAC sanctions and BIS and DoS import/export rules.

What Is a US-Origin Good?

A good is considered US origin if it is "all or virtually all" made in the United States. The origin is based on where the product was manufactured, not where it's shipped from. Items located in or passing through the US are also of US origin. Additionally, goods made outside the US that contain at least 25 percent US-origin content (10 percent for embargoed countries) or are directly made using US technology or software are also considered US origin.[108] Therefore, foreign-produced items can still be US-origin if they contain US-origin parts, technology, or software.

Other US Government Agencies That Enforce Trade Sanctions

Bureau of Industry and Security (BIS)

The US Department of Commerce's Bureau of Industry and Security (BIS) administers and enforces export controls on dual-use and military items through the Export Administration Regulations (EAR). The EAR applies to the item anywhere in the world and to foreign parties dealing with it. This includes situations where the item is reexported between foreign countries or transferred within a foreign country.

For example, an exporter cannot bypass the US embargo against Iran by shipping an item to a distributor in the United Arab Emirates.[109]

Both BIS and OFAC can impose fines on foreign companies for violating the EAR if the transaction also violates an economic sanction. For example, Alcon Laboratory in Switzerland was fined by both OFAC and BIS after selling and exporting unlicensed medical end-use surgical and pharmaceutical products from the United States to distributors in Iran and Sudan without OFAC authorization.[110]

Department of State (DoS)

The Department of State has several divisions that oversee the export of defense-related items and services under the Arms Export Control Act (AECA), the International Traffic in Arms Regulations (ITAR), and the United States Munitions List (USML). These include the Directorate of Defense Trade Controls (DDTC) and the Bureau of International Security and Non-Proliferation (ISN).

The DDTC controls commercial exports of defense articles and services. They enforce the AECA and the ITAR and can impose penalties for violations. If a company or person violates the AECA, they can be debarred, meaning they are banned from exporting defense goods and services. There are two types of debarment: statutory, which happens after a criminal conviction, and administrative, which results from a DDTC enforcement action. Debarred parties can apply for reinstatement of their export privileges after a set period.[111]

The ISN works to prevent the spread of weapons of mass destruction (WMDs), such as nuclear, chemical, and biological weapons.[112] It focuses on preventing the unauthorized trade of materials that could be used to make WMDs.

You could violate OFAC as well as BIS or DoS trade sanctions if you sell US-origin goods that require a license to sanctioned parties or sanctioned countries. The types of goods that need an export license are not always obvious. We once had a customer on the BIS list for exporting straight jackets without a license. The DoS listed another customer for sending US technology diagrams to their Chinese subsidiary for work. Although neither customer was sanctioned by OFAC, we still had to ensure we were not insuring any illegal exports from these companies to avoid violating BIS or DoS restrictions.

If you buy, sell, ship, or insure US-origin goods, both BIS and DoS have their own watchlists that you should check when screening for sanctions, in addition to the OFAC watchlists. The DoS has two watchlists: the DDTC debarred list and the ISN non-proliferation sanctions list. The BIS maintains four watchlists: two lists of users who can't receive licensable goods, one list of foreign parties subject to more restrictive licensing requirements to export goods, and one list of persons denied export privileges.

One particular advisory every foreign entity should review is the Department of Commerce, Department of the Treasury, and Department of Justice "Tri-Seal Compliance Note: Obligations of foreign-based persons to comply with US sanctions and export control laws" (link provided under Resources), which is explicitly directed at foreign companies involved in global trade.

36
What's New in Sanctions for 2025

The concepts presented in this guide will likely not change as we move forward in 2025; however, sanctions priorities and targets will. The world of economic sanctions continues to change, driven by global events and government policies. I'm not a prognosticator, and predicting specific outcomes is challenging. However, several key areas warrant close observation in the future:

Syria

Syria has been under a trade embargo for 20 years. However, with the fall of President Bashar al-Assad, sanctions on Syria are starting to shift. In the US, OFAC has issued a temporary license allowing more transactions in Syria until at least July 7, 2025. These steps suggest that sanctions could continue to ease as the situation develops.

Russia

Last year, I would have said a new administration would immediately remove many Russian sanctions. Now I'm not so sure. Many sanctions against Russia are now set in law, requiring Congress to remove them. The war in Ukraine is still going strong as of the publication date of this guide, and the new administration appears willing to use additional sanctions against Russia to end it. However, Task Force KleptoCapture, the unit responsible for tracking and seizing assets belonging to sanctioned Russian oligarchs, was disbanded. This may be part of a broader strategy to improve relations with Russia and push for an end to the war in Ukraine. Conversely, Russian sanctions are expected to tighten in other countries, especially as jurisdictions like the EU introduce more restrictions in an effort to end the Ukraine conflict.

China

China could be in the crosshairs of more serious sanctions in 2025. The new tariffs against China, the continued threat of Chinese hacking against the US, and its support of Russia could signal stronger sanctions down the road, such as increased export prohibitions. To date, there have been primarily prohibitions against investment in companies that supported the Chinese military and some technological export restrictions.

Iran and the Middle East

There may be increased sanctions pressure on Iran in 2025, especially in light of the continued conflict in the Middle East. Past actions by Trump, like pulling out of the Joint Comprehensive Plan of Action (JCPOA) and reinstating sanctions, suggest that further restrictions are likely, especially if conflicts in the region continue.

Cuba

I wouldn't expect any loosening of restrictions here. Obama relaxed some restrictions against Cuba, which were reimposed under the first Trump administration. Biden also undid some prohibitions, which were immediately reinstated by Trump when he took office for his second term, such as re-establishing the "Cuba Restricted List," which prohibits transactions with companies associated with Cuba's military, and reinstating Cuba as a State Sponsor of Terrorism.

Israel

Trump has made two key sanctions-related moves in support of Israel and Prime Minister Benjamin Netanyahu, signaling he may use sanctions during his term to help his allies.

First, he revoked Biden's Executive Order, which imposed sanctions on individuals, undermining peace, security, and stability in the West Bank. With the order repealed, all sanctioned individuals were removed from the Specially Designated Nationals (SDN) List. That same day, Israel resumed military operations in the territory.

Second, he issued a new executive order targeting the ICC, sanctioning one prosecutor under a blocking program that freezes assets and prohibits US businesses from engaging with him. This order only applies to foreign nationals—US persons cannot be sanctioned under it. However, the order expands the standard definition of a US person to include "foreign branches, subsidiaries, and employees" of US companies, broadening its reach. The move aims to deter the ICC from investigating US, Israeli, and allied nationals from countries that are not ICC member states.

It also signals that Trump may lean heavily on the International Emergency Economic Powers Act (IEEPA) to regulate international trade. Sanctions imposed under IEEPA can take effect immediately, and non-compliance carries severe penalties.

ADDITIONAL INSURANCE COMPANY CONSIDERATIONS FOR SANCTIONS

37

Economic Sanctions Considerations for Insurance

Throughout this guide, I've noted instances where insurance companies have special sanctions considerations. This chapter will cover several more sanctions issues insurance companies face when doing business globally.

Types of Insurance Affected by Sanctions

"Insurance" encompasses a wide variety of coverages that your organization may provide and may include:

- consumer insurance for home, auto, umbrella, and "toys" (such as boats or snowmobiles)
- group/employee benefits such as life, health, accidental death and dismemberment, long-term disability, and short-term disability
- commercial insurance, including property, commercial auto, general liability, product liability, workers' compensation, professional liability, employer liability, and management liability
- specialized types of insurance such as data breach/ransomware, kidnap and ransom, and flood
- travel insurance
- ocean marine

My prior company offered all of these insurance products, and each product has its own sanctions concerns, which will be covered in a later chapter.

Globality of Insurance

If you work for an insurer with only domestic (US-based) customers, your sanctions job is more manageable but not non-existent because insurance is ultimately global. The following examples illustrate this globality:

- Your company provides life insurance only to US persons. Likely, that policy will cover the policyholder anywhere in the world. So, if the covered person travels to their homeland of Iran and dies, now, you must comply with OFAC's Iran sanctions.

- Your company provides car insurance that covers car travel to Canada or Mexico. Or you provide insurance coverage for rental cars while the US policyholder is overseas. A claim could arise requiring compliance with foreign sanctions regulations.
- Your US-based business customer sells products overseas. Under a product liability policy, you may get a claim from someone in a foreign country, necessitating compliance with that country's sanctions regulations.

If you work for a foreign insurance company that offers global (i.e., worldwide) policies, your policies might have a US nexus. For example, if your company provides life insurance, that policy will likely cover the policyholder anywhere in the world, including the US. Similarly, if you offer global travel insurance, it would also cover travel to the US.

OFAC allows global coverage for life, health, and travel insurance, even in sanctioned areas, as long as the policy covers the rest of the world (meaning it cannot be specific to just one country).

However, there are some restrictions. See When Global Policies Aren't Global later in this chapter.

Multiple Jurisdictions May Be Involved

If your company offers insurance products providing coverage outside of the US, you must follow sanctions regimes in every country where you do business, which can be several jurisdictions for one policy.

An example of how this works:

Your UK subsidiary holds a Directors and Officers policy for a French-based entity doing business in Cuba and Russia.

- Your UK subsidiary wrote the policy, so there is a UK nexus.
- The customer is French, so there is an EU and French nexus.
- The customer is doing business in Cuba, giving you a US nexus, as foreign subsidiaries of US parties are considered US persons by OFAC under the Cuba program.
- The customer is doing business in Russia, a high-risk jurisdiction. The policy is subject to US, UK, and EU sanctions programs, each with subtle differences regarding Russia.

- If a covered director resides in another country, such as Japan, you must also comply with those regulations when dealing with claims related to this director.

Therefore, for one policy written in the UK, you may have to comply with US, UK, EU, Japan, and more sanctions programs, all at the same time!

Multiple Parties Involved in a Transaction

Insurance companies must be vigilant about complying with sanctions regulations when issuing policies and paying claims, as multiple parties and jurisdictions can be involved in one transaction, and all must be free of sanctions issues in order to complete the transaction. Each party must be checked to ensure compliance, and if any party is sanctioned, the transaction cannot proceed.

Here are some example scenarios where completing a transaction would be prohibited:

- An additional insured under a policy is named on the SDN (Specially Designated Nationals) list (this party would need to be excluded from coverage).
- The coverage is for property located in multiple countries, including Iran (a territorial exclusion for Iran would be needed to issue this policy).
- A non-sanctioned party includes a sanctioned bank under its credit risk policy.
- A non-sanctioned cargo company ships goods, such as oil, to or through a sanctioned party or country.
- One of several claimants under a policy is sanctioned. That claimant could not be paid, although other claimants can be as long as the sanctioned party is not the policyholder.
- A non-sanctioned individual names a beneficiary who is a sanctioned party.
- A sanctioned party wholly owns a non-sanctioned customer.

A number of these situations initially involve non-sanctioned policyholders. How should an insurance company identify and avoid these situations? The two best ways are implementing a sanctions screening program and a referral process, as discussed in Chapter 10.

When Global Policies Aren't Global

Insurers may issue policies that provide worldwide coverage, but in practice the coverage is not that comprehensive because of OFAC's sanctions programs. Depending on your customer, their industry, or the type of insurance you are providing them, you may not be able to cover certain countries or particular situations.

For example, OFAC has generally said that insurance companies can provide global, group life, health, and travel insurance worldwide.[113] But there are restrictions. If someone dies in a sanctioned country, such as Iran, the insurance proceeds can be paid to the beneficiary. But can you pay an entity in Iran for the reparation of a body back to the US? Or can you pay a foreign governmental entity to get documents related to the death? You might need to apply for a specific license in both situations. Even permissible global coverages are a bit more complicated to adhere to in practice for sanctions purposes.

Lloyd's Syndicate

Global insurance companies may participate in the Lloyd's Syndicate, as our UK subsidiary did. The Syndicate system allows multiple insurance companies to share risks for large or high-risk policies. Insurers can be the lead on a policy, hold a tier lead position, or follow the lead of another insurer. A single policy can involve twenty or more insurers. The Syndicate writes many policies involving Russia, either by writing coverage in Russia or for parties that do business there.

OFAC compliance while a member of the Lloyd's Syndicate presents its own challenges.

Since insurers in the Syndicate have different jurisdictions and ownership structures, conflicts often arise among participating insurers about whether a policy or claim violates sanctions, particularly US, UK, and EU sanctions. This is further complicated when your Syndicate underwriters claim that other insurers don't see an issue, pressuring you to follow suit.

However, neither you nor your underwriters will know the specific circumstances of each writing company, their US ownership, or how their sanctions compliance teams reached their decisions. You need to do your research, consult legal counsel when needed, document your conclusions, and stand by your decisions if conflicts occur.

For instance, we requested that Iran or Cuba be excluded territories in a policy written through the Syndicate. However, as a follow line, we often couldn't change policy wording, so if we participated, we had to rely on the sanctions exclusion language of the lead insurer. This isn't foolproof, as UK entities can legally write business involving Cuba and Iran, and as a follow line, your company may be expected to pay those claims.

In one case unresolved when I left, a claim involved an entity potentially majority-owned by a sanctioned party. We had evidence to support this and decided not to pay. The customer argued that their ownership was below 50 percent. Some insurers were willing to pay the claim; others were not.

Make the best decisions for your company's situation, and don't feel pressured to do what other insurers do.

38

Insurance Matters Complicating Sanctions Compliance

Insurance companies face various sanctions-related challenges in policy administration. Below, I outline some common issues and provide tips on effectively addressing these risks.

Third-Party Claimants

One of the tougher sanctions challenges is dealing with claimants who aren't customers of the insurance company. This often arises with third-party auto claims, where a non-customer files a claim under the customer's insurance policy. In these cases, you usually have very little information about the claimant—just a name and an address, which is often their attorney's office. If your screening system flags a potential match, it can be hard to get more details, especially if the claimant's attorney is unwilling to share information.

When this happens, we would temporarily hold the payment and ask the claims handler to try to get the needed information, like a date of birth, from the customer or their attorney. We'd let them know we couldn't process the payment until we received the information. Since people wanted their money, we usually got the details we needed or at least had more time to clear the alert through other investigative means.

Multiple Insureds

Corporate policies can cover a wide range of parties, including branch locations, subsidiaries, owners, executives, officers, directors, employees, and even third parties, like in a construction contract or bond. This information is usually found in the application and policy documents but often doesn't get into the screening system unless someone manually scans it.

To address this:
- Have the underwriter manually scan all parties to a policy.
- Work with your information technology team to create an automated process that captures all parties in the administrative system and pulls those names into a data file for your sanctions screening solution.

- Refer higher-risk policies (like those in high-risk jurisdictions) to sanctions compliance for review and scanning of all parties, as discussed in a prior chapter.

In my previous job, we used a combination of all three options, depending on whether the system could capture all parties and the potential sanctions risk of the policy.

Claims Issues

Some prohibited transactions may still slip through even with strong sanctions clauses or exclusion language in your policies. For example, you might insure a boat for hull damage, and the owner leases it to another company that takes it to Cuba, where it breaks down. Or you could cover a shipment that sinks in Crimean waters and needs local vendors to salvage it.

You can't pay a claim that would violate sanctions, but you also might be unable to deny or block it. Lloyd's recently introduced a new sanctions clause (LMA3200), which allows for suspending coverage or payment until the potential sanctions violation no longer exists. This language is becoming popular among customers. Depending on the contract terms, the claim might have to remain unresolved for years in case sanctions change and it becomes legal to pay it. Alternatively, you or the customer can apply for a specific license from OFAC to settle the claim. As always, remember the blocking statutes (discussed previously), which could complicate decisions about applying for an OFAC license.

Reinsurance

Reinsurance brings its own challenges when it comes to sanctions compliance. As a reinsurer, you're responsible for ensuring that the policies and claims you cover aren't violating sanctions, even if you don't always get the full details from the primary insurance company. Typically, you might receive a summary of premiums or claims (known as a bordereau), which may not include the names of the policyholders or claimants.

Reinsurers should request the names of policyholders and claimants, scan them, and ensure you're not providing coverage to a sanctioned party. It's possible that a policy could be legal for the primary insurance company to insure but not for you to reinsure, depending on jurisdiction. For example, a foreign insurance company may legally provide coverage to an Iranian or Cuban firm, but this could be a sanctions violation for you.

You can't rely on the primary insurance company or broker to perform the scans correctly. In one case, we found that a customer we were reinsuring was sanctioned, which was missed by the broker because they only scanned customers in sanctioned countries. This customer was in a non-sanctioned country but was owned by an Iranian entity. Always perform the scans yourself.

Start by focusing on higher-risk portfolios, like reinsurance involving clients in the Middle East or Russia, or portfolios that cover high-risk products like credit and political risk. Begin by obtaining and scanning the names of policyholders and claimants in those reinsurance contracts before moving on to less risky areas, like property coverage in European countries.

If you're unsure whether OFAC targets reinsurers, look at the case of Gen Re, which OFAC fined for paying two reinsurance claims to the Steamship Mutual Underwriting Association Limited for losses from the National Iranian Tanker Company, an SDN.[114]

Third-Party Business Partners

Insurance providers typically outsource several activities. You might outsource underwriting (to a Managing General Agent), claims handling (to a third-party administrator for life insurance policies), or information technology. Or your company could contract with a consultant to generate business. These arrangements can open you up to inadvertent sanctions violations as third parties can act independently of your sanctions requirements.

It is essential to conduct thorough due diligence on your vendors to identify higher-risk business partners up front (for ongoing monitoring) and to train them on your expectations regarding sanctions. Review Chapter 11 for how to conduct vendor due diligence.

OFAC fined one insurance company due to the actions (or inaction) of their third-party administrator (TPA).[115] The TPA managed the health insurance policies for the insurer, but neither the TPA nor the insurer scanned the names of two customers who were later added to the SDN list.

Your contract with any vendor should clearly state who is responsible for OFAC scanning. If the third party handles it, your organization should work with the third party to establish a robust sanctions screening procedure and oversee the third party's work to ensure the scans are performed correctly.

Sanctions Clause Not Allowed

In this guide, I've stressed the importance of including sanctions exclusion clauses in policies and contracts to protect your company from violations and lawsuits. However, some countries, like Israel and, to a certain extent, Japan, do not allow these clauses in their policies. If you're writing a policy in these countries, you may be unable to add a sanctions exclusion clause.

OFAC addresses this issue in FAQ #103[116] and recommends applying for a specific OFAC license to provide coverage and a separate license to pay claims. However, this process can be time-consuming and complex. It's best to work with legal counsel to develop alternative protective language that complies with the country's restrictions on sanctions clauses.

Legal Entities and Ultimate Beneficial Ownership (UBO)

As discussed in Chapter 11, UBOs can create challenges for companies. The headaches can be bigger for insurance companies, as a company's due diligence may not have identified and scanned the UBO of their legal entity customer. Recently, OFAC fined PURE Insurance for this issue.[117] Their corporate customer was wholly owned by a person who was added to the SDN list. However, PURE's scanning system only tracked the corporate customer's name, not the UBO's. As a result, the account wasn't flagged or blocked, leading to an OFAC fine.

Insurance companies will likely have many LLCs as policyholders, some of which insure high-risk assets like artwork, yachts, or luxury homes. We encountered several cases where we couldn't verify the true owners because the LLCs were layered through multiple entities established in foreign countries with weak verification controls and a lack of transparency. Later, we discovered that the ultimate owner—and thus the policyholder—was a sanctioned individual.

This highlights why insurance companies must go beyond tracking corporate clients by identifying and screening UBOs to avoid compliance violations. While insurance companies handle many types of corporate customers, it's important to have a system for collecting and verifying UBO information, especially for certain policy types (like high-value artwork) or corporate structures (like LLCs). That way, if regulators ask, you can demonstrate that you took all reasonable steps to perform due diligence.

Mergers and Acquisitions (M&A)

Insurance companies frequently buy another insurance company or a specific book of business. Sanctions compliance should always be involved in M&A discussions as they will need to assist in vetting the company for any sanctions issues. You don't want to buy a company that later gets you an OFAC fine, such as the Ace/Chubb merger.[118]

The challenges of incorporating a purchased insurance entity into your organization are too numerous to discuss in this guide. However, start with vetting the company to determine if there are or were any sanctions penalties against them, how those issues were resolved, any open investigations, what their book of business consists of (products and jurisdictions), how they screen their business, and establishing some initial oversight over those higher risk areas.

Reputational Risk

The risk to your organization's reputation from a sanctions violation might not come up often, but it's a genuine concern. Today, customers and business partners, like banks, consider more than just price—they also care about a company's ethics and reputation. Negative publicity from a sanctions issue can hurt your company's bottom line even more than an OFAC penalty.

For example, a few years ago, the US government considered naming companies, including insurance firms, involved in business related to the Nord Stream 2 pipeline, which carries natural gas from Russia and is a major revenue source for them. The US wanted work on this pipeline to cease. Eventually, they did release some names of companies that had stopped their involvement with the pipeline, including two large insurers. Although these actions weren't necessarily sanctions violations at the time for these companies, it raises the question: would you want your company named on such a list?

When reviewing policies and claims with potential sanctions issues or other negative news, bring findings to management's attention so they are fully informed before taking on a risk.

39

Specific Issues by Insurance Product

Some insurance products come with a higher risk of sanctions issues. The potential risks for a few of those products are discussed below.

Consumer Insurance

Consumer insurance is often overlooked in sanctions compliance because these policies are typically lower in value, and companies can usually collect and screen all policyholders. However, some risks still exist, so you can't skip basic sanctions procedures like scanning. Even minor violations can lead to actions from OFAC.

For example, Geico received a small fine from OFAC for providing auto insurance to a person on the SDN list. [119] While the fine was minor, the reputational damage can be more significant.

Group Employee Benefits

Your group benefits policyholder might be a company, but the claimant and underlying insureds or beneficiaries are often individuals. Should you scan all these people upfront, and what if those covered individuals change? OFAC doesn't require scanning all beneficiaries of a group policy unless you receive a list of those individuals. If you do, OFAC expects you to screen them.

OFAC has stated that if an insurer knows a person covered under a group policy is on the SDN list (which you would see if you received a list of covered employees), that person's coverage is blocked. If they file a claim, the insurer cannot pay it. If you don't know the names of the people covered under a group policy, you wouldn't need to block anything until an SDN files a claim, at which point the blocking requirement would apply. [120]

So, if you don't currently receive lists of all individuals covered under a group contract, OFAC does not require you to do so. You should implement procedures to vet those individuals at claim time.

Beneficiaries of life insurance and accidental death and dismemberment policies can be located anywhere in the world, including in sanctioned jurisdictions. As I previously described, finding a legal way to pay out some of these valid claims is difficult.

Ransomware

It's best (for you!) if your organization doesn't provide coverage for ransomware attacks, as they come with significant sanctions risks and often involve limited information about the breach or the bad actors involved. OFAC discourages paying ransoms because they usually benefit sanctioned individuals or groups, including those associated with sanctioned jurisdictions.

Ransomware attacks can involve various sanctioned entities, such as individuals, ransomware groups (which may disband and reorganize under a new name), specific ransomware versions, the ransomware's creator, or even the crypto wallet addresses used for payment.

In smaller ransom cases, your customer might pay it without hiring an incident response firm like Coveware. These firms specialize in identifying attackers, assessing the attack method, and performing initial sanctions reviews with tools that most insurance companies don't have. These firms can sometimes trace payments to their destinations, adding another layer of security.

If an incident response firm is involved, review its report to confirm what sanctions screening was conducted and its results. We did have one or two occasions where the firm recommended not paying the ransom and did not assist the customer in paying it due to a sanctions issue. If the incident response firm recommends not paying a ransom, your organization certainly should not.

If no firm is involved, your organization will need to conduct these scans, even though your customer may know little about the ransomware software used or the hacking group involved. Emails or screenshots of ransom demands may provide clues, which you can research online to identify the group behind them.

A growing trend in the insurance industry is for insurers to pay the ransom directly through a cryptocurrency operator rather than reimburse the customer. Regardless of the payment method, it still raises sanctions concerns as the insurance company will pay the ransom directly to the offender or indirectly through the customer.

Do your best to conduct thorough due diligence now and document every step taken. Even if a sanctions issue is discovered later, having detailed records of your due diligence efforts will be crucial for defending your actions with OFAC. We developed a form for each ransomware claim, which the sanctions compliance team used to document the information received on the attack, due diligence performed to identify sanctions issues, and any discussions with outside legal counsel.

Travel Insurance

As previously mentioned, global travel insurance coverage is usually allowed, but exceptions exist. Cuban travel seems to trip up insurers the most. Travel to Cuba must be under one of the authorized general licenses before an insurance company can provide coverage.

When we provided travel insurance for school groups going to Cuba, we had to conduct thorough checks to ensure compliance with these licenses by:

- Reviewing the detailed daily agenda to ensure it meets the general license terms. We denied coverage for trips with too much touristy sightseeing time.
- Obtaining a signed affidavit from the travel provider confirming that the trip met the terms of the general license (usually "support for the Cuban people" or "educational").
- Collecting and keeping the names of all travelers going to Cuba.

If you don't follow these rules when providing travel insurance for trips to Cuba, you risk facing OFAC fines. For example, one US insurance company was fined by OFAC because their Canadian branch, considered a US person by OFAC, issued travel insurance policies that occasionally covered Canadian residents traveling to Cuba.[121]

Ocean Marine

Marine insurance is one of the highest-risk areas when it comes to sanctions, mainly because of all the moving parts involved. There are many parties to keep track of, including the shipper, receiver, consignee, freight forwarder, ultimate beneficiary, the ship (including its owner and crew company), agents, goods (oil —be careful complying with the Russia oil price cap sanctions), and shipment routes (is the route going through a sanctioned jurisdiction?). Whether you're insuring the ship itself or the goods being transported, each party needs to be identified and checked against sanctions lists. Some insurers even check the names of the ship's crew.

The situation is further complicated because some shipping firms are skilled at evading detection. They might briefly turn off their AIS (Automated Identification System) tracker to move goods to banned locations like Russia or North Korea. Alternatively, oil tankers may transfer oil from one ship to another at sea to avoid detection, with the final destination being a sanctioned country.

A strong sanctions exclusion clause in your policy is crucial to managing these risks. Detailed due diligence on claims is also essential. This might include checking the certificate of origin for goods or reviewing the ship's route to ensure it didn't pass through any prohibited areas or experience periods when the AIS was turned off.

OFAC fined one insurance company because it insured shipments transhipping or destined for a sanctioned country.[122]

Credit and Political Risk

These types of policies typically are at higher risk for sanctions as well. Credit risk may have counterparties that may not be known until claim time. There could also be claimants in sanctioned jurisdictions, or part of the transaction has a nexus to a sanctioned country.

We had a foreign financial institution customer with a credit risk policy. The institution held a portfolio of bonds. The financial institution was sued for not properly managing the bonds, resulting in losses to the investors. It came to us for payment under the policy. Unfortunately, two of the portfolio's bonds were Cuban government bonds, and we were advised we couldn't pay the claim.

In a second instance, a company filed a claim under the credit risk policy when their customer defaulted on a loan. Unfortunately, their customer had recently been sanctioned, which led to the default, and we could not pay the claim since it involved an SDN.

40
Conclusion

In the ever-evolving landscape of global commerce, navigating economic sanctions can be complex. However, with the knowledge and strategies outlined in this guide, you now have the tools to manage sanctions risks effectively and ensure compliance with regulations set forth by the Office of Foreign Assets Control (OFAC).

Throughout this book, you've learned how economic sanctions work and the key compliance issues. You've discovered how to develop a sanctions compliance program, conduct a risk assessment, and ensure your business complies with evolving regulations. You've gained insights into screening transactions, identifying red flags, and handling potential violations. By applying these key skills, you can protect your company from costly penalties, safeguard its reputation, and confidently operate in the global marketplace.

In the ever-evolving world of economic sanctions, staying informed is essential. Sanctions can shift frequently, even weekly. What's acceptable today might not be tomorrow, as new programs and watchlists are regularly introduced or revised. With the knowledge gained from this guide, alongside other available resources, staying informed about sanctions is manageable. By being proactive, you can navigate the complex sanctions landscape with confidence.

Remember, compliance isn't just about avoiding fines but about upholding ethical and legal standards while navigating a complex global landscape. By adhering to sanctions regulations, your organization contributes to international stability and security, fostering a safer and more transparent economic environment.

Effective communication and collaboration across the company is essential. Companies can ensure policies are practical, executable, and aligned with business objectives by involving key stakeholders in developing and implementing sanctions compliance procedures. This collaborative approach fosters buy-in from employees at all levels and promotes a culture of compliance.

Additionally, leveraging technology and automation can streamline sanctions compliance processes and enhance efficiency. Technology offers valuable resources for managing compliance obligations effectively, from sanctions screening tools to automated reporting systems. By harnessing its power, companies can improve accuracy, reduce manual errors, and stay ahead of evolving regulatory requirements.

With dedication, diligence, and a commitment to excellence, you can build and sustain a robust sanctions program that safeguards your company's interests and promotes ethical business practices in today's interconnected world.

41

Test Your Knowledge

It is time to test your knowledge of what was presented in this guide.

Questions

1. You want to purchase Cuban cigars. Can you pay a company in Cuba to buy these cigars?
    a. Would your answer change if you sent money to your father in Cuba rather than purchasing Cuban cigars?
2. You work for a US-based company that wants to sign a contract to sell products to the Government of Venezuela. Can you do this business?
    a. Would your answer change if you worked for the foreign branch of the US-based company?
    b. Would your answer change if you worked for the foreign subsidiary of the US-based company?
    c. Would your answer to (b) change if you wanted to do business with an Iranian company instead?
3. Match the type of sanction to its definition.
    a. List Based
    b. Comprehensive
    c. Sectoral
       **
    1. Trade Embargo
    2. Specially Designated Nationals (SDN) list
    3. Industry sanctions
4. Your company wants to do business with A Russian Company, an entity on the Sectoral Sanctions Identifications (SSI) list. Can you do business with them?
    a. No. They are sanctioned, so we can't do business with them.
    b. Possibly, depending on the business we want to do with them.
    c. Yes. The SSI list is a non-SDN sanctions list, so we can do business with them.

5. You have a new business consultant, Jose Morales, in Texas. Do you need to scan this person through the OFAC lists?
   a. Yes.
   b. No. He's a US person, so he wouldn't be sanctioned.

6. Referring back to Question #5, you scan Jose Morales and discover he's a match to an SDN of the same name in Mexico. What do you do?
   a. Nothing. My potential business partner is in Texas, and the SDN is in Mexico.
   b. Refuse to do business with him and report him to OFAC.
   c. Obtain more information on my potential business partner to see if it matches the SDN information provided by OFAC.

7. You are a foreign entity with a new business consultant, Tyler Newsome, in Canada, who will generate some business for you in North America. Do you need to scan this person against the OFAC lists?
   a. Yes.
   b. No. There is no US nexus to this relationship.

8. Your insurance company is asked to provide townhome insurance to Oligarch Property Management, LLC. The management company is listed as the owner of the property. You scan the management company, and it is not sanctioned. However, you learn by talking to one of the employees that the beneficial owner of the property is a Russian person. When you scan the name, you find out he is sanctioned by the US and the UK. Can you provide this insurance?
   a. No. A sanctioned party is the beneficial owner of the property.
   b. Yes. Our customer is the management company, which isn't sanctioned.

9. You want to do business with XYZ Company in the UK. You know XYZ Company is a subsidiary of a Russian energy company. You scan XYZ Company through the OFAC lists, and they are not on the SDN list. Are you clear to do business with them?
   a. No
   b. Yes
   c. Not yet

10. A firm in Russia wants to buy your computer technology. You know OFAC prohibits the export of computer technology to Russia. Are any of the following responses appropriate:
    a. You can't sell it to them, but you refer the Russian company to a foreign firm that sells that technology.
    b. You sell it to them through one of your foreign subsidiaries.
    c. You arrange to sell the technology to a third party in another country, which then sells it to them.

11. A Canadian firm with a branch in Russia wants your US-based insurance company to provide liability insurance to its entire organization. OFAC sanctioned the Russian branch. Are any of the following responses appropriate?
    a. You can't issue the policy through your US writing company, but refer it to your UK subsidiary to write.
    b. You can write the policy if there is a territorial exclusion for Russia and the Russian branch.
    c. You can't issue the policy because one of the branches is sanctioned, which means the entire organization is sanctioned.

12. Your company has the opportunity to do business with an entity in Yemen, but you see Yemen has an OFAC sanctions program. Can you do this business?
    a. Yes
    b. No

13. You work for a US-based insurance company, and your US customer filed a claim to be reimbursed for the repair of her Persian rug. She sent her rug to Iran for repair. Can you pay this claim?
    a. Yes. Our customer is a US person and has not been sanctioned.
    b. No.

14. You provide group life insurance to a corporate customer. They provide you with a list of all employees. Do you have to scan this list to ensure no employees are SDNs?
    a. No. The corporation is our customer.
    b. Yes. OFAC expects that if you have the names, you scan them.

15. You provide Directors and Officers insurance to a global company. There is a claim under the policy for a director. When you scan the director's name, you find they were recently sanctioned. What do you do?
    a. Pay the claim directly to the non-sanctioned global company.
    b. Deny the claim.
    c. Block the claim payment.

16. You are a US branch of an Indian company. Your customer wants to buy your sonar equipment for a party in Russia. You recognize that OFAC regulations prohibit exporting this equipment to Russia. Are any of your responses below appropriate?
    a. Refer the business to your parent company in India, as they may be able to make the sale.
    b. Complete the transaction using a wholesaler in China, which does not prohibit the export of your sonar equipment to Russia.
    c. Decline the business as you are considered a US person, and this transaction would violate OFAC.

17. You work for a foreign branch of a US-based accounting firm. Your branch wants to do business with XYZ Company, a Russian energy company. You scan XYZ Company, and they are not on the SDN list. Are you clear to do business with them?
    a. No
    b. Yes
    c. Not yet

18. You work for a foreign company not considered a US person. You are conducting a sale of your video games to a company in Syria. After completing the transaction, you discovered that you sent payment through a foreign bank that used a US correspondent account to complete the transaction. What do you do?
    a. This is likely a violation of OFAC as a US financial institution was used during the sales process. Discuss with management whether to self-report this violation to OFAC.

b. Do nothing. There is no OFAC violation to this transaction. You sent the transaction through a foreign bank, not the US correspondent bank.

19. You work for a foreign financial institution with no US ties that has a Russian aerospace customer. Do you have an OFAC issue with this account?

   a. No. There is no US nexus.

   b. Yes. This could be a violation of OFAC's secondary sanctions.

20. Your company is a freight forwarder located in Germany facilitating a shipment of medical supplies from the US to India. You scan all parties involved in the shipment and discover the vessel is sanctioned. Can you conduct this shipment?

   a. No. A party to the shipment is sanctioned, so the entire transaction is prohibited.

   b. Yes. Our customer is not sanctioned.

   c. Yes. It involves medical supplies, which fall under a humanitarian general license.

Answers

1. No, you cannot purchase Cuban cigars online from someone in Cuba and cannot send money there for commercial purposes.
   a. Yes, you can send money to your father using the personal remittance general license.
2. No, the Government of Venezuela is sanctioned by OFAC.
   a. No, foreign branches are US persons subject to OFAC regulations for all sanctions programs.
   b. Maybe. The foreign subsidiary may be able to do this business as it is not subject to OFAC regulations. However, verify there is no US nexus to the transaction and implement a recusal policy for US personnel.
   c. Yes, the answer to (b) would change. Under Iranian regulations, the foreign subsidiary is a US person and thus could not do this business either.
3. A-2, B-1, C-3
4. B. If your potential customer is on OFAC's SSI list, you may still be able to do business with them, as only specific activities are prohibited. If they are subject to sectoral sanctions for debt or equity restrictions, transactions unrelated to issuing or purchasing debt or equity may be allowed, provided they comply with those restrictions. However, be aware that a commercial transaction could inadvertently involve the issuance of debt if payment terms extend credit to the sanctioned party longer than what is allowed by the restriction. To stay compliant, ensure payment terms do not exceed the time limit set by the restrictions. On the other hand, if you want to sell A Russian Company computer parts, it's likely to be a prohibited transaction that you cannot conduct.
5. A. You have to scan anyone you do business with through OFAC, no matter where they are located, as anyone anywhere in the world, including the US, can be on the SDN list.
6. C. Usually, obtaining further information on your potential business partner, such as their Social Security Number, Date of Birth, or address

history, that you can compare to the party on the SDN list should clear this potential match. You are not yet required to refuse to do business with him and report him to OFAC (choice B) since you haven't confirmed whether you have a positive match. Choice A is also incorrect, as people can move, and the fact that the SDN is located in Mexico doesn't mean he could not have moved recently to the US.

7. A. You have to scan a new business partner who may be generating US-related business for you through OFAC, no matter where they are located, as OFAC can sanction anyone anywhere in the world.

8. A. The beneficial owner of the townhome you are asked to insure is sanctioned. In effect, the townhome is "frozen" by its sanctioned ownership, and you can't provide services, such as insurance, for it.

9. C. Knowing a Russian company owns it and it operates in an industry subject to sanctions, you should also scan the Russian owner through OFAC. If they are sanctioned and own 50 percent or more of XYZ Company, then XYZ Company is deemed sanctioned, and you either can't do business with them or do certain transactions with them.

10. All of these alternatives are fraught with potential sanctions violations. Referring a firm to another company that may be able to provide a service you cannot due to OFAC sanctions could be considered facilitation. Depending on OFAC's secondary sanctions concerning Russia and computer technology and the sanctions in the country where the foreign subsidiary is located, you might not be allowed to sell through a foreign subsidiary. Arranging to sell via a third party to an SDN is considered an indirect transaction and a violation.

11. B is the best response. As long as that sanctioned branch is excluded from coverage, you should be able to insure the rest of the company. Referring a firm to your subsidiary that may be able to provide a service you cannot due to OFAC sanctions could be considered facilitation (choice A), and the entire company is not sanctioned just by virtue of a branch being sanctioned (choice C).

12. A. Yes, you can do business with this entity in Yemen if it is not on the OFAC list. Yemen is a list-based sanctions program, meaning OFAC only

prohibits doing business with parties on the SDN list, not with Yemen as a country.

13. B. You cannot reimburse your customer for this expense. The customer had the rug repaired in Iran and paid an Iranian company for the work. As a commercial entity, your insurance company would indirectly provide funds to the Iranian company by reimbursing the claim, which OFAC prohibits.

14. B. Yes, OFAC expects that you would have scanned the names if you have them. However, if the company did not provide you with the roster of covered employees, you do not have to request and scan them.

15. C. You cannot pay a claim involving a sanctioned party, even if the insured is not sanctioned. However, you also cannot deny the claim if it's valid. In this case, you may need to reject the transaction if the funds are considered the property of the company rather than the sanctioned individual. If the funds belong to the sanctioned director, you must block the payment (if the claim was processed before they became an SDN), apply for an OFAC license to pay the claim, or let the claim remain unresolved until sanctions change, allowing you to complete the process.

16. C. You must decline the business as you are considered a US person, and this transaction would violate OFAC. Referring the business to your parent company in India (choice A) is considered facilitation by OFAC and is illegal. Remember, US persons are not allowed to refer business to another company that they themselves cannot conduct. Completing the transaction using a wholesaler in China (choice B) would indirectly supply the goods to Russia, which OFAC also considers a sanctions violation.

17. C. Knowing they are a Russian company and that the US has prohibited providing accounting services to entities within Russia, you likely cannot provide the service. However, there are exceptions to review first. Would the services be provided to a subsidiary in another country? Is the Russian entity owned or controlled by a US person? In those situations, you may be able to provide the service.

18. A. This is likely an OFAC violation. The fact that the payment went through a US correspondent bank account, even though your company did

not send it through the account directly, still gave the transaction a US nexus, and most transactions with Syria are prohibited.

19. B. Being a foreign financial institution (FFI) with an account for a Russian aerospace company could violate Executive Order 14024, which imposes secondary sanctions on FFIs doing business with Russian SDNs in specific industries and any persons operating in certain sectors, such as aerospace. You should consider divesting yourself of that account.

20. A. A party to the transaction (in this case, the vessel) is sanctioned by OFAC, so the entire transaction is prohibited. Just because your customer is not sanctioned (choice B) doesn't mean the transaction is legal. A humanitarian general license (choice C) is not applicable as India, the ultimate destination, is not a sanctioned jurisdiction and has no general licenses available. However, you can continue the shipment if you use a non-sanctioned vessel.

References

Below is a good reference list of websites with further details on the information provided in this guide.

All OFAC Sanctions Programs
https://ofac.treasury.gov/sanctions-programs-and-country-information

OFAC Frequently Asked Questions
https://ofac.treasury.gov/faqs/all-faqs

Free OFAC List Search Tool
https://sanctionssearch.ofac.treas.gov/

OFAC Compliance Guidance for Sanctions Programs
https://ofac.treasury.gov/media/16331/download?inline

UK Sanctions Programs
https://www.gov.uk/government/collections/financial-sanctions-regime-specific-consolidated-lists-and-releases

EU Sanctions Programs
https://www.sanctionsmap.eu/#/main

OFAC Enforcement Actions
https://ofac.treasury.gov/civil-penalties-and-enforcement-information

Department of Commerce, Department of the Treasury, and Department of Justice Tri-Seal Compliance Note: Obligations of foreign-based persons to comply with US sanctions and export control laws
https://www.justice.gov/opa/media/1341411/dl?inline

Bureau of Industry and Security Lists of Parties of Concern
https://www.bis.doc.gov/index.php/policy-guidance/lists-of-parties-of-concern/entity-list

US Department of State, Directorate of Defense Trade Controls https://www.pmddtc.state.gov/ddtc_public/ddtc_public

US Department of State, Bureau of International Security and Nonproliferation
https://www.state.gov/bureaus-offices/under-secretary-for-arms-control-and-international-security-affairs/bureau-of-international-security-and-nonproliferation/

Consolidated Screening List
https://www.trade.gov/consolidated-screening-list

United Nations Sanctions
https://main.un.org/securitycouncil/en/sanctions/information

Federal Financial Institutions Examination Council (FFIEC), BSA/AML Manual, Appendix J: Quantity of Risk Matrix
https://bsaaml.ffiec.gov/manual/Appendices/11

FFIEC, BSA/AML Manual, Risk Assessment
https://bsaaml.ffiec.gov/manual/BSAAMLRiskAssessment/01

Artic Intelligence, Sanctions Risk
https://arctic-intelligence.com/risk-domains/sanctions#

Audit Board, Risk Assessment Matrix: Overview and Guide
https://www.auditboard.com/blog/what-is-a-risk-assessment-matrix/

ACAMS Today, Keeping Sanctions-Related Risk Assessments Effective and Current
https://www.acamstoday.org/keeping-sanctions-related-risk-assessments-effective-and-current/

Sanctions Scanner
https://sanctionscanner.com/knowledge-base/office-of-foreign-assets-control-ofac-274

Edward J. Collins-Chase, "Sanctions Primer: How the United States Uses Restrictive Mechanisms to Advance Foreign Policy or National Security Objectives" (Congressional Research Service, 2023), https://crsreports.congress.gov/product/pdf/R/R47829

Author Biography

Heidi Hunter worked for a US-based insurance company with global operations for over a decade. She developed and managed the company's sanctions compliance program, covering all its locations. She oversaw the team responsible for complying with sanctions and worked closely with other teams within the company to ensure they understood and followed sanctions regulations. Heidi has a Master of Business Administration (MBA) and is a Certified Public Accountant (inactive).

Visit her website at https://easysanctions.wordpress.com/ for more information on sanctions and to sign up for her newsletter.

All Books in the Plain-English Guide Series by Heidi Hunter

The Plain-English Guide to Economic Sanctions

The Plain-English Guide to Developing an Economic Sanctions Program

The Plain-English Guide to Economic Sanctions Risk Assessments

The Plain-English Guide to Economic Sanctions for Insurance Companies

The Plain-English Guide to Economic Sanctions for Foreign Companies

The Plain-English Guide to Economic Sanctions: The Complete Series

Companion Workbooks:

The Plain-English Guide to Developing an Economic Sanctions Program Workbook

The Plain-English Guide to Economic Sanctions Risk Assessments Workbook

Find them all at: https://books2read.com/ap/xdZrqL/Heidi-Hunter

If you read one of my guides, please post a rating or review!

Notes

1. OFAC, Frequency Asked Questions, FAQ 12, https://ofac.treasury.gov/faqs/12.

2. Due to the end of Bashar al-Assad's regime, on January 6, 2025, OFAC issued General License 24, expanding authorizations for activities and transactions in Syria for an initial six-month period, effective until July 7, 2025. This may lead to the permanent loosening of comprehensive sanctions against Syria.

3. OFAC, FAQ 986.

4. FFIEC, "FFIEC BSA/AML Examination Manual," Politically Exposed Persons, November 2021, https://www.ffiec.gov/press/PDF/Politically-Exposed-Persons.pdf.

5. OFAC, FAQ 18.

6. OFAC, Frequently Asked Questions, FAQ 3, https://ofac.treasury.gov/faqs/all-faqs.

7. OFAC, FAQ 3.

8. European Union Sanctions, https://www.eeas.europa.eu/eeas/european-union-sanctions_en.

9. Edward J Collins-Chase, "Sanctions Primer: How the United States Uses Restrictive Mechanisms to Advance Foreign Policy or National Security Objectives" (Congressional Research Service, 2023), https://crsreports.congress.gov/product/pdf/R/R47829.

10. OFAC, Lebanon-Related Sanctions page, https://ofac.treasury.gov/sanctions-programs-and-country-information/lebanon-related-sanctions.

11. OFAC, Russian Harmful Foreign Activities Sanctions page, https://ofac.treasury.gov/sanctions-programs-and-country-information/russian-harmful-foreign-activities-sanctions.

12. *Code of Federal Regulations*, Title 31, Subpart B, Chapter V, Part 549 Lebanese Sanctions Regulations, https://www.ecfr.gov/current/title-31/subtitle-B/chapter-V/part-549?toc=1.

13. OFAC, Afghanistan-Related Sanctions page, https://ofac.treasury.gov/sanctions-programs-and-country-information/afghanistan-related-sanctions.

14. OFAC, FAQ 886.

15. OFAC, FAQ 11.

16. OFAC, "OFAC Settles with Swedbank Latvia for $3,430,900 Related to Apparent Violations of Sanctions on Crimea," June 26, 2023, https://ofac.treasury.gov/media/931911/download?inline.

17. OFAC, "OFAC Settles with Toll Holdings Limited for $6,131,855 Related to Apparent Violations of Multiple Sanctions Programs," April 25, 2022, https://ofac.treasury.gov/media/922441/download?inline.

18. "What are Secondary Sanctions?" Dow Jones Risk & Compliance Glossary, accessed April 25, 2024, https://www.dowjones.com/professional/risk/glossary/sanctions/secondary-sanctions/.

19. OFAC, "Re-Imposition of the Sanctions on Iran That Had Been Lifted or Waived Under the JCPOA," November 4, 2018, https://ofac.treasury.gov/sanctions-programs-and-country-information/iran-sanctions/re-imposition-of-the-sanctions-on-iran-that-had-been-lifted-or-waived-under-the-jcpoa.

20. Executive Order 14114, "Taking Additional Steps with Respect to the Russian Federation's Harmful Activities," December 22, 2023, https://ofac.treasury.gov/media/932441/download?inline.

21. OFAC "Treasury Sanctions Investors Supporting Assad Regime's Corrupt Reconstruction Efforts," June 17, 2020, https://home.treasury.gov/news/press-releases/sm1037 (Nader Kalai and Luxury Tourism Section).

22. *Code of Federal Regulations*, Cuban Asset Control Regulations, 31 CFR§ 515.329, https://www.ecfr.gov/current/title-31/subtitle-B/chapter-V/part-515?toc=1.

23. *Code of Federal Regulations*, Iranian Transactions and Sanctions Regulations, 31 CFR§ 560.215, https://www.ecfr.gov/current/title-31/subtitle-B/chapter-V/part-560?toc=1.

24. *Code of Federal Regulations*, "North Korea Sanctions Regulations," 31 C.F.R §510.214, https://www.ecfr.gov/current/title-31/subtitle-B/chapter-V/part-510/subpart-B/section-510.214.

25. OFAC, FAQ 10.

26. "Overview of US Sanctions," Wilkie Compliance, accessed April 25, 2024, https://complianceconcourse.willkie.com/resources/sanctions-us-overview-of-us-sanctions/.

27. Edward J Collins-Chase, "Sanctions Primer: How the United States Uses Restrictive Mechanisms to Advance Foreign Policy or National Security Objectives" (Congressional Research Service, 2023), https://crsreports.congress.gov/product/pdf/R/R47829.

28. *Code of Federal Regulations*, Global Magnitsky Sanctions Regulations, 31 CFR Part 583, https://www.ecfr.gov/current/title-31/subtitle-B/chapter-V/part-583/subpart-B/section-583.201.

29. *Code of Federal Regulations*, Global Magnitsky Sanctions Regulations.

30. OFAC, Other OFAC Sanctions Lists, https://ofac.treasury.gov/other-ofac-sanctions-lists; OFAC, FAQ 91.

31. OFAC, Ukraine-/Russia-related Sanctions, https://ofac.treasury.gov/sanctions-programs-and-country-information/ukraine-russia-related-sanctions.

32. OFAC, "Directive 1 (As Amended on September 29, 2017) Under Executive Order 13662", https://ofac.treasury.gov/media/8696/download?inline.

33. OFAC, Other Lists, Non-SDN Menu Based Sanctions List, https://ofac.treasury.gov/other-ofac-sanctions-lists.

34. Executive Order 14059 of December 15, 2021, "Imposing Sanctions on Foreign Persons Involved in the Global Illicit Drug Trade," https://ofac.treasury.gov/media/917361/download?inline.

35. OFAC, "Determination Pursuant To Section 1(A)(Ii) of Executive Order 14024," https://ofac.treasury.gov/media/926586/download?inline.

36. OFAC, FAQ 1061.

37. OFAC, "Determination Pursuant To Section 1(A)(Ii) of Executive Order 14071, Prohibitions Related to Certain Quantum Computing Services," https://ofac.treasury.gov/media/926591/download?inline.

38. OFAC, FAQ 1061.

39. Executive Order 14068, "Prohibiting Certain Imports, Exports, and New Investment with Respect to Continued Russian Federation

Aggression," March 11, 2022, https://ofac.treasury.gov/media/919281/download?inline.

40. Executive Order 14066 "Prohibiting Certain Imports and New Investments with Respect to Continued Russian Federation Efforts To Undermine the Sovereignty and Territorial Integrity of Ukraine," March 8, 2022, https://ofac.treasury.gov/media/919111/download?inline.

41. OFAC, Determination Pursuant to Section 1(a)(i)(A) of Executive Order 14068, "Prohibitions Related to Imports of Aluminum, Copper, and Nickel of Russian Federation Origin," https://ofac.treasury.gov/media/932796/download?inline.

42. Bureau of Industry and Security, Common High Priority List, https://www.bis.gov/articles/russia-export-controls-list-common-high-priority-items.

43. OFAC, FAQ 91.

44. Executive Order 13884, "Blocking Property of the Government of Venezuela," August 5, 2019, https://ofac.treasury.gov/media/26786/download?inline.

45. OFAC, FAQ 91.

46. Department of the Treasury, "Revised Guidance on Entities Owned by Persons Whose Property and Interests in Property Are Blocked," https://ofac.treasury.gov/media/6186/download?inline; OFAC, FAQ 399.

47. Scott Patterson and Ian Talley, "Sanctioned Russian Oligarch Deripaska Distances Himself From Rusal", *Wall Street Journal,* April 27, 2018, https://www.wsj.com/articles/russian-tycoon-oleg-deripaska-to-sell-majority-stake-in-en-group-1524848098.

48. Department of the Treasury, "A Framework for OFAC Compliance Commitments," https://ofac.treasury.gov/media/16331/download?inline.

49. Department of the Treasury, "A Framework for OFAC Compliance Commitments."

50. Department of the Treasury, "A Framework for OFAC Compliance Commitments."

51. Department of the Treasury, "A Framework for OFAC Compliance Commitments."

52. Department of the Treasury, "OFAC Issues a Finding of Violation to MidFirst Bank for Violations of the Weapons of Mass Destruction

Proliferators Sanctions Regulations", July 21, 2022, https://ofac.treasury.gov/media/924506/download?inline.

53. FinCEN, Beneficial Ownership Information, Frequently Asked Questions, https://www.fincen.gov/boi-faqs.

54. OFAC, FAQ 102.

55. Lloyds Market Association Bulletin LMA23-028-AR, "Sanctions Clauses," October 5, 2023, https://www.lmalloyds.com/LMA_Bulletins/LMA23-028-AR.aspx.

56. EU Council Regulation (E.C.) No 2271/96 of November 22, 1996, as amended by Commission Delegated Regulation (E.U.) 2018/1100 of June 6, 2018, https://www.legislation.gov.uk/eur/1996/2271; "Spotlight on the U.K. Protection of Trading Interests Legislation," Wilkie Compliance, accessed April 25, 2024, https://complianceconcourse.willkie.com/resources/sanctions-uk-uk-blocking-statute/.

57. Debevoise and Plimpton, "UK High Court Rules on Sanctions Clauses in Insurance Contracts and Considers Application of the EU Blocking Regulation," October 30, 2018, https://www.debevoise.com/-/media/files/insights/publications/2018/10/20181030_uk_high_court_rules_on_sanctions_clauses_in_insurance_contracts_and_considers_application_of_the_eu_blocking_regulation.pdf.

58. Debevoise and Plimpton, "UK High Court Rules on Sanctions Clauses in Insurance Contracts and Considers Application of the EU Blocking Regulation."

59. Baker McKenzie, "Sanctions clauses and US extraterritorial sanctions – Lamesa v Cynergy appeal," July 10, 2020, https://sanctionsnews.bakermckenzie.com/sanctions-clauses-and-us-extraterritorial-sanctions-lamesa-v-cynergy-appeal/.

60. Royal Court of Justice, The Court of Appeal (Civil Division), Judgment, "Lamesa Investments Limited and Cynergy Bank Limited," June 30, 2020, https://www.judiciary.uk/wp-content/uploads/2020/07/Lamesa-v-Cynergy.APPROVED-JUDGMENTS.pdf.

61. Wilmer Hale, "Top EU Court Rules on the EU Blocking Regulation Against US Sanctions for the First Time," January 31, 2022, https://www.wilmerhale.com/insights/client-alerts/20220124-top-eu-court-rules-on-the-eu-blocking-regulation-against-us-sanctions-for-the-first-time.

62. Department of the Treasury, "A Framework for OFAC Compliance Commitments."

63. Department of the Treasury, "A Framework for OFAC Compliance Commitments."

64. Department of the Treasury, "A Framework for OFAC Compliance Commitments."

65. Department of the Treasury, "A Framework for OFAC Compliance Commitments."

66. Department of the Treasury, "A Framework for OFAC Compliance Commitments."

67. Department of the Treasury, "e.l.f Cosmetics, Inc Settles Potential Civil Liability for Apparent Violations of the North Korea Sanctions Regulations," January 21, 2019, https://ofac.treasury.gov/media/7041/download?inline.

68. Department of the Treasury, "e.l.f Cosmetics, Inc Settles Potential Civil Liability for Apparent Violations of the North Korea Sanctions Regulations," January 21, 2019, https://ofac.treasury.gov/media/7041/download?inline.

69. Auditboard, Risk Assessment Matrix: Overview and Guide," accessed June 18, 2024, https://www.auditboard.com/blog/what-is-a-risk-assessment-matrix/.

70. Vcomply, "What is a Risk Assessment Matrix? How to Create One?" accessed July 11, 2024, https://www.v-comply.com/blog/what-is-risk-assessment-matrix.

71. *BSA/AML Manual*, Appendix J: Quantity of Risk Matrix, Federal Financial Institutions Examination Council (FFIEC), accessed May 8, 2024, https://bsaaml.ffiec.gov/manual/Appendices/11.

72. OFAC, "OFAC Risk Matrix," Economic Sanctions Enforcement Guidelines, 31 C.F.R Part 501, Appendix A, Annex, https://www.ecfr.gov/current/title-31/subtitle-B/chapter-V/part-501/appendix-Appendix_A_to_Part_501.

73. OFAC, Sanctions Programs and Country Information, https://ofac.treasury.gov/sanctions-programs-and-country-information.

74. FATF, "Black and Grey Lists," accessed May 20, 2024, https://www.fatf-gafi.org/en/countries/black-and-grey-lists.html.

75. Transparency International, Corruption Perceptions Index, accessed May 20, 2024, https://www.transparency.org/en/cpi/2023.

76. United States Drug Enforcement Administration, High Intensity Drug Trafficking Areas, https://www.dea.gov/operations/hidta; The White House, "High Intensity Drug Trafficking Areas Program," https://www.whitehouse.gov/wp-content/uploads/2023/06/HIDTA-map-May-2023.pdf.

77. Financial Crimes Enforcement Network, HIFCA Regional Map, https://www.fincen.gov/hifca-regional-map; Comply Advantage, "What Are High Intensity Financial Crime Areas (HIFCAs), https://complyadvantage.com/insights/hifcas/.

78. FFIEC, BSA/AML Manual, Office of Foreign Assets Control, Office of Foreign Assets Control—Overview, accessed May 17, 2024, https://bsaaml.ffiec.gov/manual/OfficeOfForeignAssetsControl/01.

79. Wikipedia, "Five Whys" accessed on June 13, 2024, https://en.wikipedia.org/wiki/Five_whys.

80. OFAC, FAQ 9.

81. OFAC, FAQ 9.

82. OFAC, FAQ 63.

83. OFAC, FAQ 49.

84. OFAC, FAQ 8.

85. OFAC, "Supplemental Guidance for The Provision of Humanitarian Assistance," February 27, 2023, https://ofac.treasury.gov/media/931341/download?inline; FAQ 1105.

86. OFAC, "United Medical Instruments Inc Settles Potential Civil Liability for Alleged Violations of the Iranian Transactions and Sanctions Regulations," February, 28, 2017, https://ofac.treasury.gov/media/11181/download?inline.

87. OFAC, FAQs 227, 243, 453, 462, 732.

88. OFAC, FAQ 74.

89. OFAC, FAQ 905.

90. *Code of Federal Regulations*, 31 CFR § 501.601 - Records and recordkeeping requirements, https://www.ecfr.gov/current/title-31/subtitle-B/chapter-V/part-501/subpart-C/section-501.601.

91. Baker McKenzie, "OFAC Issues Interim Final Rule Regarding 10-Year Recordkeeping Requirement," October 9, 2024, https://sanctionsnews.bakermckenzie.com/ofac-issues-interim-final-rule-regarding-10-year-recordkeeping-requirement.

92. OFAC, FAQ 12.

93. Department of the Treasury, "Treasury Announces $508 Million Settlement with British American Tobacco Largest Ever Against Non-Financial Institution," April 25, 2023, https://home.treasury.gov/news/press-releases/jy1441.

94. Department of the Treasury, Enforcement Release, "OFAC Settles with Binance Holdings, Ltd for $968,618,825 Related to Apparent Violations of Multiple Sanctions Programs," November 21, 2023, https://ofac.treasury.gov/media/932351/download?inline.

95. Department of Justice, Office of Public Affairs, Press Release, "US Citizen Who Conspired to Assist North Korea in Evading Sanctions Sentenced to Over Five Years and Fined $100,000," April 12, 2022, https://www.justice.gov/opa/pr/us-citizen-who-conspired-assist-north-korea-evading-sanctions-sentenced-over-five-years-and.

96. EU Council Regulation (E.C.) No 2271/96 of November 22, 1996, as amended by Commission Delegated Regulation (E.U.) 2018/1100 of June 6, 2018, https://www.legislation.gov.uk/eur/1996/2271; "Spotlight on the U.K. Protection of Trading Interests Legislation," Wilkie Compliance, accessed April 25, 2024, https://complianceconcourse.willkie.com/resources/sanctions-uk-uk-blocking-statute/.

97. *Code of Federal Regulations*, Iraq Stabilization and Insurgency Sanctions Regulations, § 576.315, https://www.ecfr.gov/current/title-31/subtitle-B/chapter-V/part-576/subpart-C/section-576.315.

98. OFAC, "Alfa Laval Middle East Ltd Settles Potential Civil Liability for Apparent Violations of the Iranian Transactions and Sanctions Regulations," July 19, 2021, https://ofac.treasury.gov/media/911521/download?inline.

99. *Code of Federal Regulations*, § 560.208, Iranian Transactions and Sanctions Regulations, Prohibited Facilitation by United States Persons of Transactions by Foreign Persons, https://www.ecfr.gov/current/title-31/subtitle-B/chapter-V/part-560/subpart-B/section-560.208.

100. OFAC, "Alfa Laval Inc Settles Potential Civil Liability for Apparent Violations of the Iranian Transactions and Sanctions Regulations," July 19, 2021, https://ofac.treasury.gov/media/911516/download?inline.

101. Department of Commerce, Department of the Treasury, and Department of Justice, "Tri-Seal Compliance Note: Obligations of foreign-based persons to comply with US sanctions and export control laws," March 6, 2024, https://www.justice.gov/opa/media/1341411/dl?inline.

102. OFAC, "CSE Global Limited and CSE TransTel Pte Ltd Settle Potential Civil Liability for Apparent Violations of the International Emergency Economic Powers Act and the Iranian Transactions and Sanctions Regulations," July 27, 2017, https://ofac.treasury.gov/media/11186/download?inline.

103. OFAC, "Wells Fargo Bank, N.A Settles Potential Liability for Apparent Violations of the Foreign Narcotics Kingpin Sanctions Regulations," June 27, 2013, https://ofac.treasury.gov/media/13661/download?inline.

104. OFAC, "Alfa Laval Middle East Ltd Settles Potential Civil Liability for Apparent Violations of the Iranian Transactions and Sanctions Regulations," https://ofac.treasury.gov/media/911521/download?inline.

105. OFAC, "Stanley Black & Decker, Inc Settles Potential Civil Liability for Apparent Violations of the Iranian Transactions and Sanctions Regulations Committed by its Chinese-Based Subsidiary Jiangsu Guoqiang Tools Co Ltd.," March 27, 2019, https://ofac.treasury.gov/media/13911/download?inline.

106. OFAC, "Guidance on the Provision of Certain Services Relating to the Requirements of US Sanctions Laws," January 12, 2017, https://ofac.treasury.gov/media/6211/download?inline.

107. OFAC, "OFAC Settles with Cameron International Corporation for Its Potential Civil Liability for Apparent Violations of Ukraine-Related Sanctions Regulations," September 27, 2021, https://ofac.treasury.gov/media/913321/download?inline.

108. Department of Commerce, Department of the Treasury, and Department of Justice "Tri-Seal Compliance Note: Obligations of foreign-based persons to comply with US sanctions and export control laws," March 6, 2024, https://www.justice.gov/opa/media/1341411/dl?inline.

109. Department of Commerce, Department of the Treasury, and Department of Justice Tri-Seal Compliance Note.

110. OFAC, "Alcon Laboratories, Inc., Alcon Pharmaceuticals Ltd., and Alcon Management, SA, Settle Potential Civil Liability for Apparent Violations of the Iranian Transactions and Sanctions Regulations and the Sudanese Sanctions Regulations," July 5, 2016, https://ofac.treasury.gov/media/11641/download?inline.

111. US Department of State, Directorate of Defense Trade Controls, Defense Trade Controls Compliance (DTCC), accessed on October 27, 2024, https://www.pmddtc.state.gov/ddtc_public/ddtc_public?id=ddtc_kb_article_page&sys_id=000d7b84dbc7bf0044f9ff621f9619a3.

112. US Department of State, Bureau of International Security and Nonproliferation, accessed on October 27, 2024, https://www.state.gov/bureaus-offices/under-secretary-for-arms-control-and-international-security-affairs/bureau-of-international-security-and-nonproliferation/.

113. OFAC, FAQ 776.

114. OFAC, Gen Re Settles Iranian Transactions Regulations Allegations, June 29, 2011, https://ofac.treasury.gov/media/13836/download?inline.

115. OFAC, "AXA Equitable Life Insurance Company Receives a Finding of Violation Regarding Violations of the Foreign Narcotics Kingpin Sanctions Regulations," August 2, 2016, https://ofac.treasury.gov/media/11666/download?inline.

116. OFAC, FAQ 103.

117. OFAC, "OFAC Settles with Privilege Underwriters Reciprocal Exchange for $466,200 Related to Apparent Violations of the Ukraine-/Russia-Related Sanctions Regulations," December 21, 2023, https://ofac.treasury.gov/media/932486/download?inline.

118. OFAC, "Chubb Limited (as Successor Legal Entity of the Former ACE Limited) Settles Potential Liability for Apparent Violations of the Cuban Assets Control Regulations," December 9, 2019, https://ofac.treasury.gov/media/25921/download?inline.

119. OFAC, "GEICO General Insurance Company Settles Foreign Narcotics Kingpin Sanctions Regulations Allegations," June 3, 2010, https://ofac.treasury.gov/media/13131/download?inline.

120. OFAC, FAQ 64.

121. OFAC, "Allianz Global Risks US Insurance Company Settles Potential Liability for Apparent Violations of the Cuban Assets Control Regulations," December 19, 2019, https://ofac.treasury.gov/media/25926/download?inline.

122. OFAC, "American International Group, Inc Settles Potential Liability for Apparent Violations of Multiple Sanctions Programs," June 26, 2017, https://ofac.treasury.gov/media/11141/download?inline.

www.ingramcontent.com/pod-product-compliance
Lightning Source LLC
Chambersburg PA
CBHW060500030426
42337CB00015B/1663